Skills for Effective Writing 2

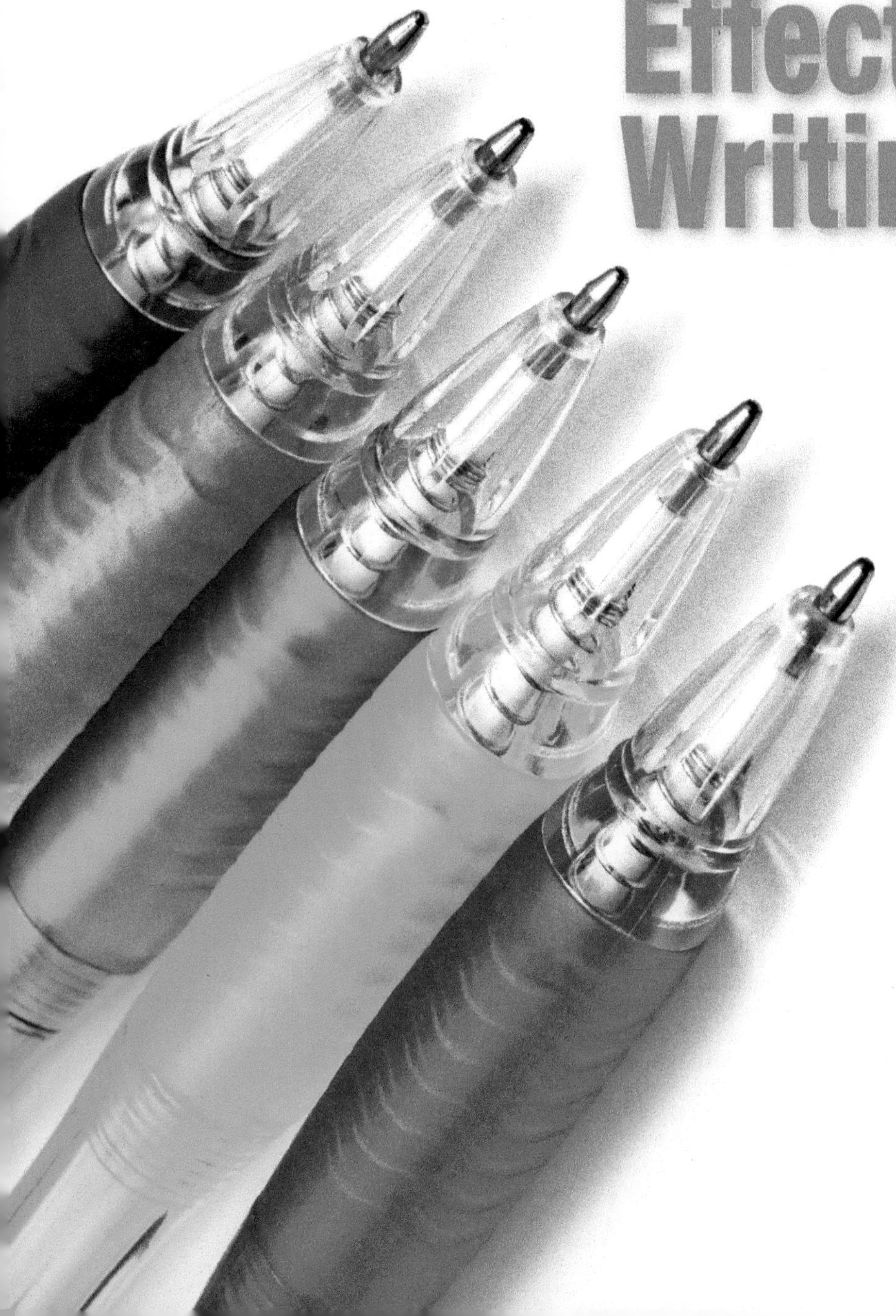

CAMBRIDGE
UNIVERSITY PRESS

CAMBRIDGE
UNIVERSITY PRESS

University Printing House, Cambridge CB2 8BS, United Kingdom

One Liberty Plaza, 20th Floor, New York, NY 10006, USA

477 Williamstown Road, Port Melbourne, VIC 3207, Australia

314–321, 3rd Floor, Plot 3, Splendor Forum, Jasola District Centre, New Delhi – 110025, India

79 Anson Road, #06–04/06, Singapore 079906

Cambridge University Press is part of the University of Cambridge.

It furthers the University's mission by disseminating knowledge in the pursuit of education, learning and research at the highest international levels of excellence.

www.cambridge.org
Information on this title: www.cambridge.org/9781107613539

First published 2013
Reprinted 2018

Printed in Italy by Rotolito S.p.A.

A catalogue record for this publication is available from the British Library

ISBN 978-1-107-61353-9 Student's Book

The publisher wishes to acknowledge the contributions of the following writers: Neta Simpkins Cahill, Susan Hills, Hilary Hodge, Elizabeth Iannotti, Robyn Brinks Lockwood, Kathryn O'Dell, and Caren Shoup.

Art direction, book design, cover design, editorial management, layout services, and photo research: Hyphen S.A.

Cover image: ©Ingmar Bjork/Shutterstock.com

Photography: 2 ©Stephen Coburn/Shutterstock.com; 6 ©YAKOBCHUK VASYL/Shutterstock.com; 10 ©Monkey Business Images/ Shutterstock.com; 14 ©mangostock/Shutterstock.com; 18 ©VIPDesignUSA/Shutterstock.com; 22 ©Hemera/Thinkstock.com; 26 ©PureStock/Superstock.com; 30 ©iofoto/ Shutterstock.com; 34 ©Vixit/Shutterstock.com; 38 ©lightpoet/Shutterstock.com; 42 ©Phase4Photography/Shutterstock.com; 46 ©gary718/Shutterstock.com; 50 ©Jon Feingersh/Superstock.com; 54 ©MBI/Superstock.com; 58 ©Dallas Events Inc/ Shutterstock.com; 62 ©robophobic/Shutterstock.com; 66 ©Kuzma/Shutterstock.com; 70 ©Lisa F. Young/Shutterstock.com; 74 ©sukiyaki/Shutterstock.com; 78 ©Andresr/Shutterstock.com; 82 ©StockLite/Shutterstock.com; 86 ©Jorge Salcedo/ Shutterstock.com; 90 ©YAKOBCHUK VASYL/Shutterstock.com; 94 ©Franck Boston/Shutterstock.com; 98 ©Otna Ydur/Shutterstock.com; 102 ©Lifesize/ Thinkstock.com; 106 ©Wendy Kaveney Photography/Shutterstock.com; 110 ©mmaxer/Shutterstock.com; 114 ©SVLuma/Shutterstock.com; 118 ©Diego Cervo/Shutterstock.com; 122 ©DPiX Center/Shutterstock.com; 126 ©qingqing/ Shutterstock.com

Skills for Effective Writing 2

CAMBRIDGE
UNIVERSITY PRESS

Contents

Skill Walkthrough

Discrete writing skills, such as creating topic sentences and recognizing irrelevant information, are critical for good writers. This 4-level series teaches these skills and offers extensive practice opportunities.

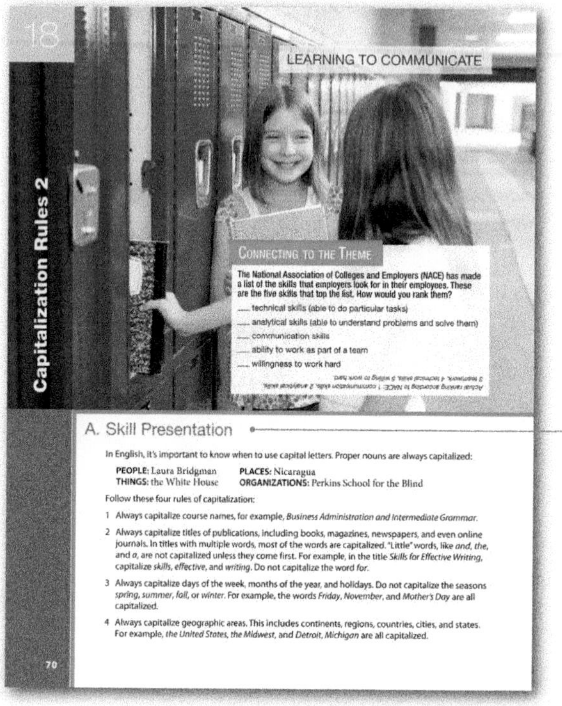

18

LEARNING TO COMMUNICATE

Capitalization Rules 2

CONNECTING TO THE THEME

The National Association of Colleges and Employers (NACE) has made a list of the skills that employers look for in their employees. These are the five skills that top the list. How would you rank them?

___ technical skills (able to do particular tasks)
___ analytical skills (able to understand problems and solve them)
___ communication skills
___ ability to work as part of a team
___ willingness to work hard

Actual ranking according to NACE: 1 communication skills, 2 analytical skills, 3 teamwork, 4 technical skills, 5 willing to work hard.

A. Skill Presentation

In English, it's important to know when to use capital letters. Proper nouns are always capitalized:

PEOPLE: Laura Bridgman **PLACES:** Nicaragua
THINGS: the White House **ORGANIZATIONS:** Perkins School for the Blind

Follow these four rules of capitalization:

1 Always capitalize course names, for example, *Business Administration and Intermediate Grammar*.
2 Always capitalize titles of publications, including books, magazines, newspapers, and even online journals. In titles with multiple words, most of the words are capitalized. "Little" words, like *and, the,* and *a*, are not capitalized unless they come first. For example, in the title *Skills for Effective Writing*, capitalize *skills, effective*, and *writing*. Do not capitalize the word *for*.
3 Always capitalize days of the week, months of the year, and holidays. Do not capitalize the seasons *spring, summer, fall*, or *winter*. For example, the words *Friday, November*, and *Mother's Day* are all capitalized.
4 Always capitalize geographic areas. This includes continents, regions, countries, cities, and states. For example, *the United States, the Midwest*, and *Detroit, Michigan* are all capitalized.

70

Skill Presentation

Each unit teaches a single discrete writing skill, helping students focus their attention on developing the skill fully.

Over to You

Following instruction, students are eased into the skill's application, facilitating their understanding of exactly how each skill works.

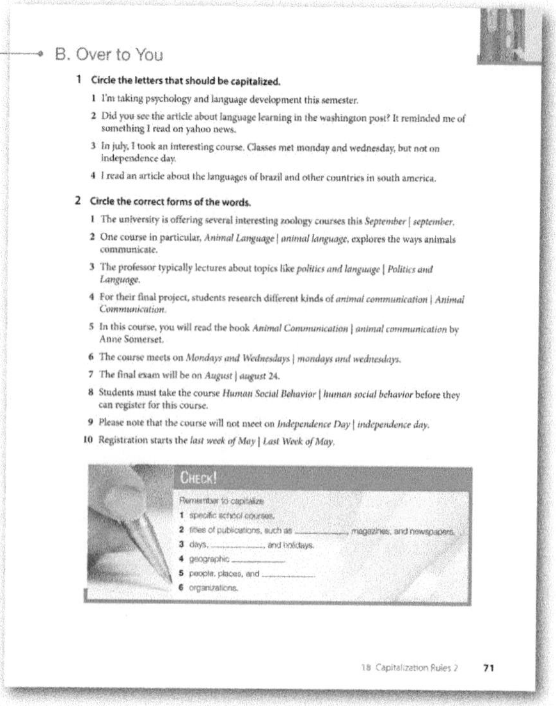

B. Over to You

1 Circle the letters that should be capitalized.

1 I'm taking psychology and language development this semester.
2 Did you see the article about language learning in the washington post? It reminded me of something I read on yahoo news.
3 In july, I took an interesting course. Classes met monday and wednesday, but not on independence day.
4 I read an article about the languages of brazil and other countries in south america.

2 Circle the correct forms of the words.

1 The university is offering several interesting zoology courses this *September | september*.
2 One course in particular, *Animal Language | animal language*, explores the ways animals communicate.
3 The professor typically lectures about topics like *politics and language | Politics and Language*.
4 For their final project, students research different kinds of *animal communication | Animal Communication*.
5 In this course, you will read the book *Animal Communication | animal communication* by Anne Somerset.
6 The course meets on *Mondays and Wednesdays | mondays and wednesdays*.
7 The final exam will be on *August | august* 24.
8 Students must take the course *Human Social Behavior | human social behavior* before they can register for this course.
9 Please note that the course will not meet on *Independence Day | independence day*.
10 Registration starts the *last week of May | Last Week of May*.

CHECK!

Remember to capitalize

1 specific school courses.
2 titles of publications, such as ________, magazines, and newspapers.
3 days, ________, and holidays.
4 geographic ________
5 people, places, and ________
6 organizations.

18 Capitalization Rules 2 71

When students master these skills, all of their writing improves. This allows teachers to focus their time and feedback on the content of student work.

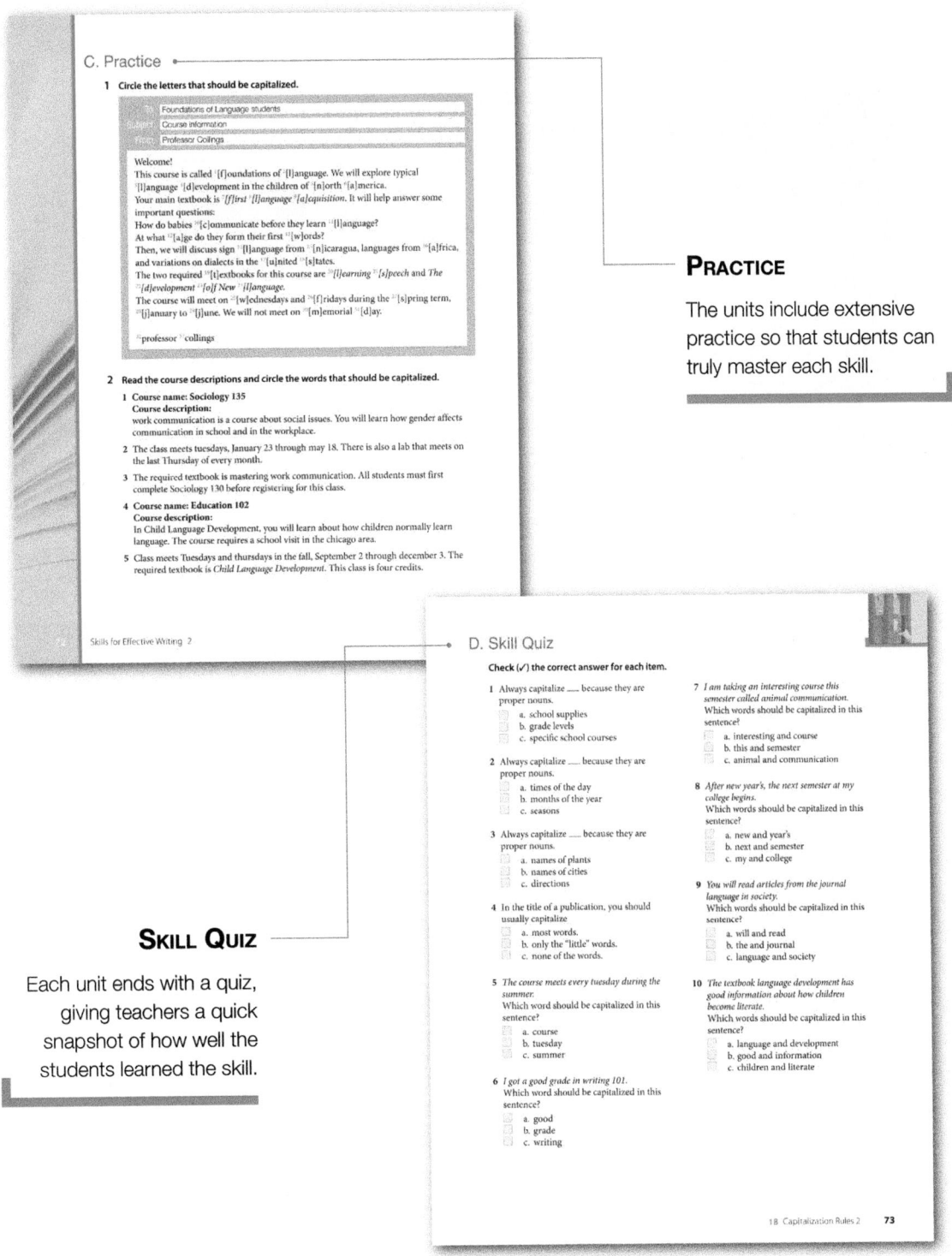

C. Practice

1 Circle the letters that should be capitalized.

To: Foundations of Language students
Subject: Course information
From: Professor Collings

Welcome!
This course is called [1][f]oundations of [2][l]anguage. We will explore typical [3][l]anguage [4][d]evelopment in the children of [5][n]orth [6][a]merica.
Your main textbook is [7]*[f]irst* [8]*[l]anguage* [9]*[a]cquisition*. It will help answer some important questions:
How do babies [10][c]ommunicate before they learn [11][l]anguage?
At what [12][a]ge do they form their first [13][w]ords?
Then, we will discuss sign [14][l]anguage from [15][n]icaragua, languages from [16][a]frica, and variations on dialects in the [17][u]nited [18][s]tates.
The two required [19][t]extbooks for this course are [20]*[l]earning* [21]*[s]peech* and *The* [22]*[d]evelopment* [23]*[o]f New* [24]*[l]anguage*.
The course will meet on [25][w]ednesdays and [26][f]ridays during the [27][s]pring term, [28][j]anuary to [29][j]une. We will not meet on [30][m]emorial [31][d]ay.

[32]professor [33]collings

2 Read the course descriptions and circle the words that should be capitalized.

1 **Course name: Sociology 135**
Course description:
work communication is a course about social issues. You will learn how gender affects communication in school and in the workplace.

2 The class meets tuesdays, January 23 through may 18. There is also a lab that meets on the last Thursday of every month.

3 The required textbook is mastering work communication. All students must first complete Sociology 130 before registering for this class.

4 **Course name: Education 102**
Course description:
In Child Language Development, you will learn about how children normally learn language. The course requires a school visit in the chicago area.

5 Class meets Tuesdays and thursdays in the fall, September 2 through december 3. The required textbook is *Child Language Development*. This class is four credits.

Skills for Effective Writing 2

Practice

The units include extensive practice so that students can truly master each skill.

D. Skill Quiz

Check (✓) the correct answer for each item.

1 Always capitalize ___ because they are proper nouns.
- a. school supplies
- b. grade levels
- c. specific school courses

2 Always capitalize ___ because they are proper nouns.
- a. times of the day
- b. months of the year
- c. seasons

3 Always capitalize ___ because they are proper nouns.
- a. names of plants
- b. names of cities
- c. directions

4 In the title of a publication, you should usually capitalize
- a. most words.
- b. only the "little" words.
- c. none of the words.

5 *The course meets every tuesday during the summer.*
Which word should be capitalized in this sentence?
- a. course
- b. tuesday
- c. summer

6 *I got a good grade in writing 101.*
Which word should be capitalized in this sentence?
- a. good
- b. grade
- c. writing

7 *I am taking an interesting course this semester called animal communication.*
Which words should be capitalized in this sentence?
- a. interesting and course
- b. this and semester
- c. animal and communication

8 *After new year's, the next semester at my college begins.*
Which words should be capitalized in this sentence?
- a. new and year's
- b. next and semester
- c. my and college

9 *You will read articles from the journal language in society.*
Which words should be capitalized in this sentence?
- a. will and read
- b. the and journal
- c. language and society

10 *The textbook language development has good information about how children become literate.*
Which words should be capitalized in this sentence?
- a. language and development
- b. good and information
- c. children and literate

18 Capitalization Rules 2 73

Skill Quiz

Each unit ends with a quiz, giving teachers a quick snapshot of how well the students learned the skill.

1

Simple Sentences

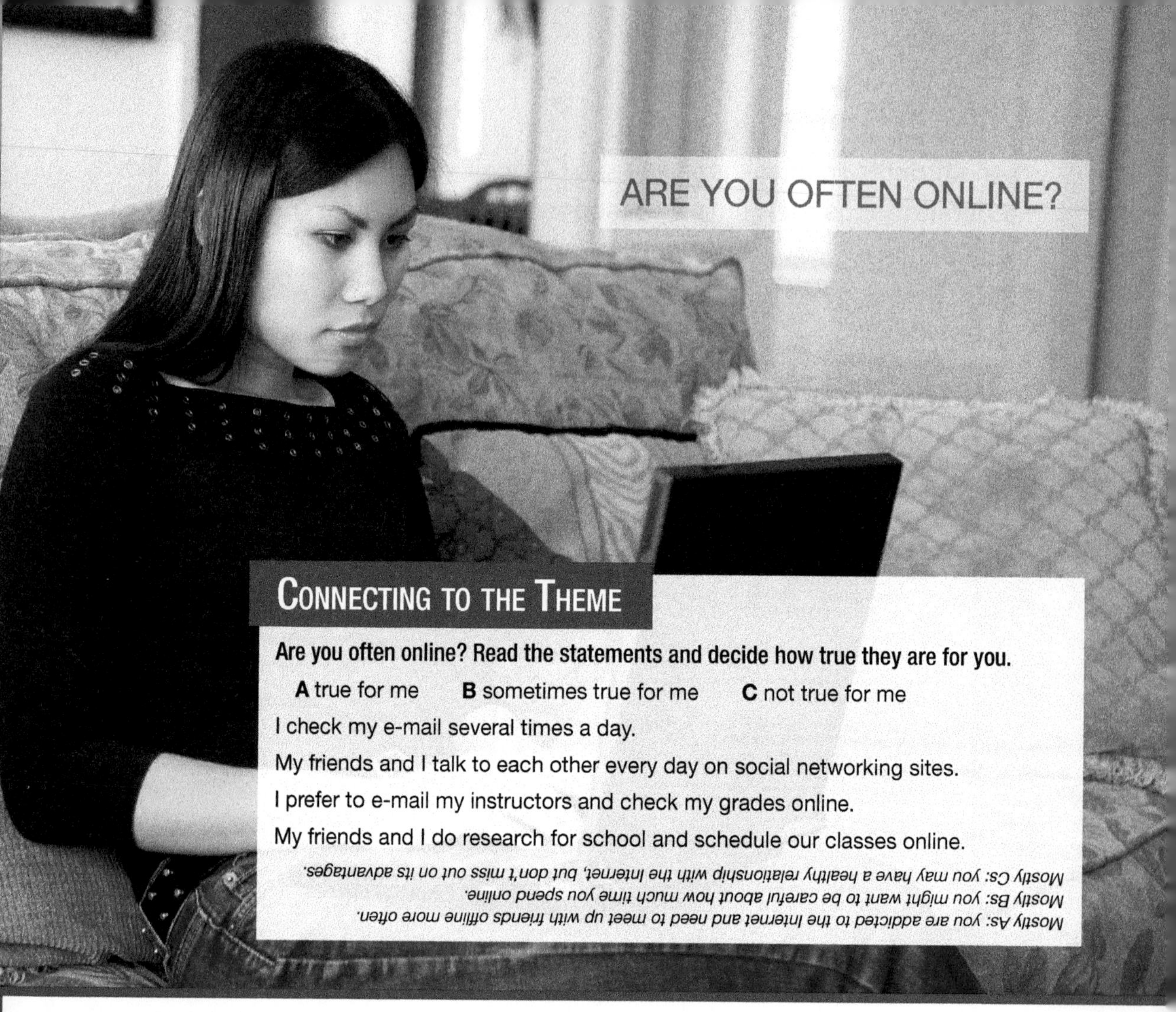

ARE YOU OFTEN ONLINE?

Connecting to the Theme

Are you often online? Read the statements and decide how true they are for you.

A true for me **B** sometimes true for me **C** not true for me

I check my e-mail several times a day.

My friends and I talk to each other every day on social networking sites.

I prefer to e-mail my instructors and check my grades online.

My friends and I do research for school and schedule our classes online.

Mostly As: you are addicted to the Internet and need to meet up with friends offline more often.
Mostly Bs: you might want to be careful about how much time you spend online.
Mostly Cs: you may have a healthy relationship with the Internet, but don't miss out on its advantages.

A. Skill Presentation

A sentence is a group of words that makes a complete idea. Every sentence needs a **subject** and a **verb**.

There are four types of simple sentences (the **S** stands for *subject*, and the **V** stands for *verb*):

1 An SV sentence has one subject and one verb. **SV = 1 subject + 1 verb**

Marina likes social networking sites.
(The subject is *Marina*. The verb is *likes*.)

2 An SSV sentence has two subjects and one verb. **SSV = 2 subjects + 1 verb**

David and **Amy like** online shopping.
(The two subjects are *David* and *Amy*. The verb is *like*.)

3 An SVV sentence has one subject and two verbs. **SVV = 1 subject + 2 verbs**

Mike usually **checks** the weather and **sends** e-mails every morning.
(The subject is *Mike*. The two verbs are *checks* and *sends*.)

4 An SSVV sentence has two subjects and two verbs. **SSVV = 2 subjects + 2 verbs**

Laura and **Pedro shopped** for books and **searched** for classes online.
(The two subjects are *Laura* and *Pedro*. The two verbs are *shopped* and *searched*.)

B. Over to You

1 How many subjects and how many verbs are there in each sentence? Circle the correct type of simple sentence.

1 Katarina and Mary found a new site about relationships.

SV SSV SVV SSVV

2 Pedro bought a book online and wrote about it on his blog.

SV SSV SVV SSVV

2 Read each sentence in the chart. Write the subjects and verbs in the correct column.

	SUBJECT(S)	VERB(S)
1. A recent study looked at the most popular websites for young people.		
2. Ten-year-old children usually watch TV shows and play online games.		
3. Preteens and teens like social networking sites.		
4. Clara and Nubia chat online and send messages to their friends.		
5. Many Americans spend a lot of time on e-mail.		
6. I looked at your new marketing site last night and posted a comment.		
7. My study group and I used a number of online resources for our research project.		
8. You can reconnect with old school friends on this website.		
9. I found an old friend online last night and sent her a message.		
10. My dad and I read the same blog and post comments every Saturday.		

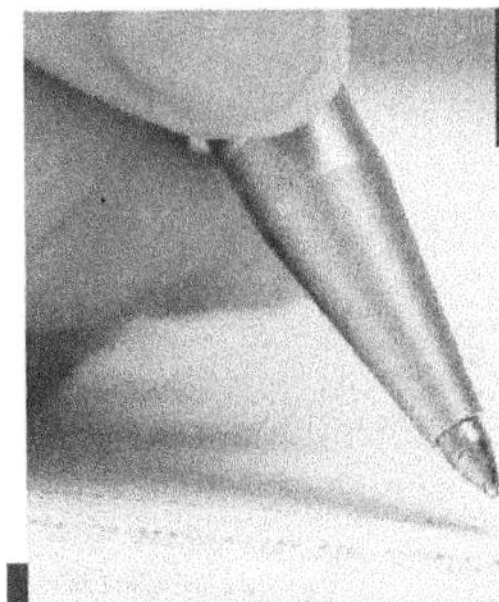

CHECK!

The four types of simple sentences are:

1 ____________ = 1 subject + 1 verb

2 ____________ = 2 subjects + 1 verb

3 ____________ = 1 subject + 2 verbs

4 ____________ = 2 subjects + 2 verbs

C. Practice

1 Read the e-mail and decide if the words in bold are subjects or verbs. Write *S* for Subject and *V* for Verb.

To: Cathy
Subject: Yesterday's conference
From: Marisela

Hi Cathy,
I [1]**went** to a technology conference yesterday. I [2]**saw** a lot of presentations and [3]**met** some nice people. [4]**Maria and Tim** [5]**were** there, too. [6]**Dr. Langman** gave an interesting presentation. She and I [7]**disagree** about a few things. [8]**She** [9]**talked** about the Internet's negative effect on everyday life. I don't think the Internet is that bad. People still [10]**interact** with each other. Dr. Langman recommends turning off technology in order to reconnect with friends. Let's talk soon.

Take care,
Marisela

1 ___ **3** ___ **5** ___ **7** ___ **9** ___
2 ___ **4** ___ **6** ___ **8** ___ **10** ___

2 Read each sentence and decide what type of simple sentence it is. Write *SV*, *SSV*, *SVV*, or *SSVV*.

___ **1** The average American spends 32.7 hours online every week.
___ **2** Technology and Sociology are my two classes this semester.
___ **3** Sandra and her mother shopped online.
___ **4** Most people talk to friends and share photos online.
___ **5** Maria and Juan usually study in the library and eat lunch in the park.
___ **6** The Internet affects our lives.
___ **7** Many teenagers meet friends at school and interact with them online.
___ **8** Many adults enjoy social networking sites.
___ **9** John and his wife pay their bills and book their vacations on the Internet.
___ **10** Alejandra goes to a tutoring session and practices the piano after school.

D. Skill Quiz

Check (✓) the correct answer for each item.

1 A sentence is a group of words that makes

- [ ] a. a person.
- [ ] b. an example.
- [ ] c. a complete idea.
- [ ] d. an action.

2 A subject is often

- [ ] a. a noun.
- [ ] b. a preposition.
- [ ] c. an adjective.
- [ ] d. an adverb.

3 Which word is a verb?

- [ ] a. Mr. Brown
- [ ] b. online
- [ ] c. sociologist
- [ ] d. meet

4 *My sister and I are friends on a social networking site.*
What type of sentence is this?

- [ ] a. SV
- [ ] b. SSV
- [ ] c. SVV
- [ ] d. SSVV

5 *Carol and Tom usually interact online and spend time together offline.*
What type of sentence is this?

- [ ] a. SV
- [ ] b. SSV
- [ ] c. SVV
- [ ] d. SSVV

6 *Teenagers interact with their friends on social networking sites.*
What type of sentence is this?

- [ ] a. SV
- [ ] b. SSV
- [ ] c. SVV
- [ ] d. SSVV

7 *Juliet searched for health information and took it to her doctor.*
What type of sentence is this?

- [ ] a. SV
- [ ] b. SSV
- [ ] c. SVV
- [ ] d. SSVV

8 *Music blogs and restaurant review sites are my two favorite types of websites.*
What type of sentence is this?

- [ ] a. SV
- [ ] b. SSV
- [ ] c. SVV
- [ ] d. SSVV

9 *Betty and Alex stayed home and spent time online.*
What type of sentence is this?

- [ ] a. SV
- [ ] b. SSV
- [ ] c. SVV
- [ ] d. SSVV

10 *Many ten-year-olds enjoy video games.*
What type of sentence is this?

- [ ] a. SV
- [ ] b. SSV
- [ ] c. SVV
- [ ] d. SSVV

2

What Is a Paragraph?

BRAINPOWER

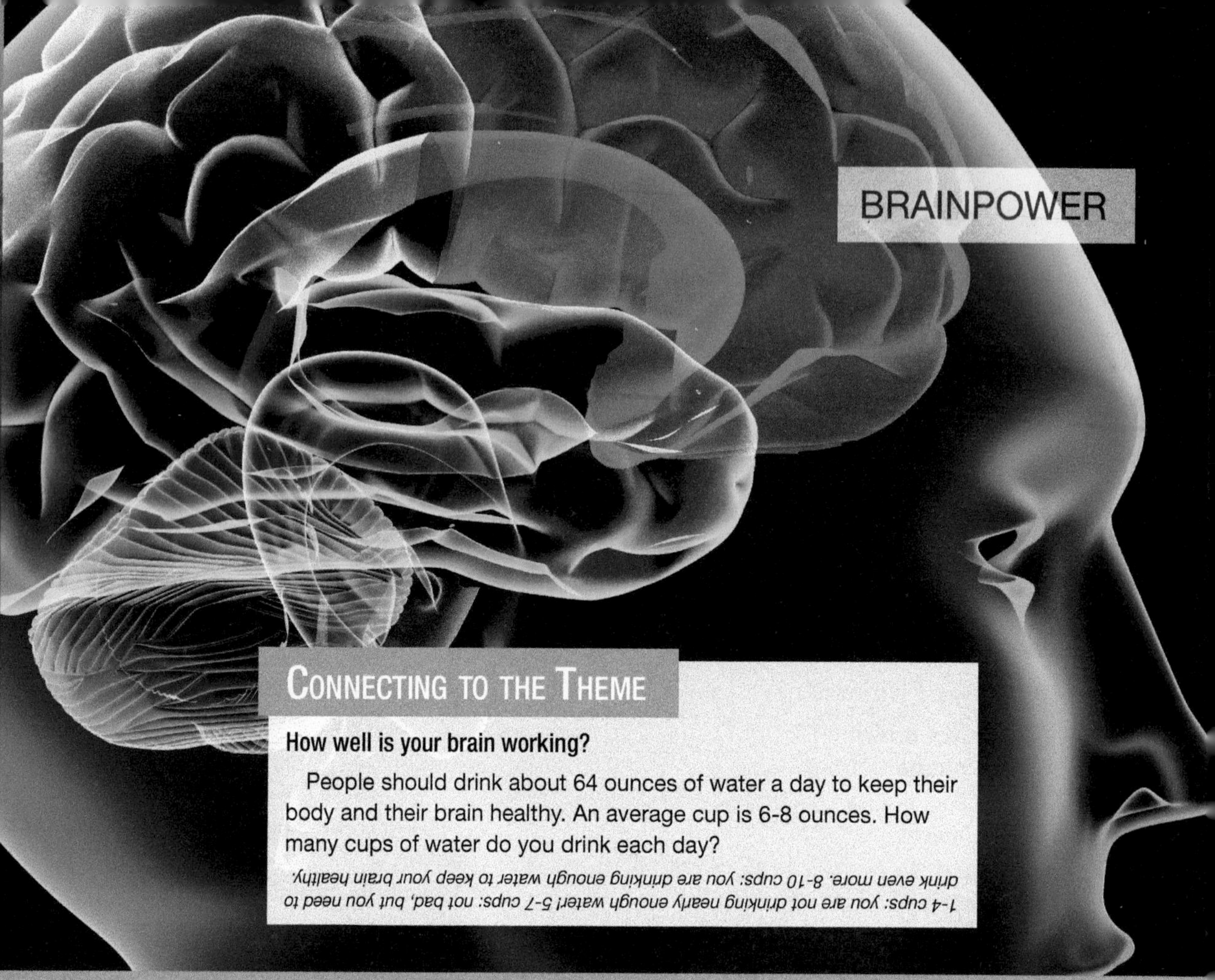

Connecting to the Theme

How well is your brain working?

People should drink about 64 ounces of water a day to keep their body and their brain healthy. An average cup is 6-8 ounces. How many cups of water do you drink each day?

1-4 cups: you are not drinking nearly enough water! 5-7 cups: not bad, but you need to drink even more. 8-10 cups: you are drinking enough water to keep your brain healthy.

A. Skill Presentation

A **paragraph** has several sentences about one topic. The first sentence in a paragraph states the main idea. The other sentences support that idea and give more information.

Paragraph

- **Main idea**
- **Supporting sentences**
- **Concluding sentence**

Read this paragraph. The topic is the importance of water for your brain.

> MYour brain needs a lot of water to work properly. SIf you don't drink enough water, your body takes it from your brain. SThis can cause a headache. CDrink plenty of water to help your brain and avoid a headache.

Always use correct paragraph formatting.

- Indent the first sentence of each paragraph. To indent means to add space before the first word. Only indent the first line of a paragraph.
- Do not start each new sentence on a new line. Sentences continue on the same line, one after the other. Only start a new line when you start a new paragraph.
- After each sentence, leave a space between the period and the first word of the next sentence. If you are using a computer, type one or two spaces after the period. Some people type one space; some people type two spaces.

B. Over to You

1 Check (✓) the paragraph with the correct formatting.

☐ 1 Scientists study the brain to understand why some things make us happy.They can test us to see how our brains respond to happy situations.
They can also see that some people's brains do not respond to happy situations.They hope that this will help them understand why some people are often unhappy.

☐ 2 Scientists study the brain to understand why some things make us happy. They can test us to see how our brains respond to happy situations. They can also see that some people's brains do not respond to happy situations. They hope that this will help them understand why some people are often unhappy.

2 Match each sentence (1–6) with a sentence (a–h) from the same paragraph.

___ 1 What we eat has an effect on brain health.

___ 2 There are activities that harm our brains.

___ 3 When you have an exam, it is a good idea to prepare your brain.

___ 4 Some experts believe that stress makes the brain weaker.

___ 5 Sometimes we remember things clearly, but other times we cannot remember things well at all.

___ 6 You can improve your brain power in several ways.

___ 7 Someone with a low IQ score can still have a successful career.

___ 8 It is important to protect your brain from injury.

a They think that people who worry less may have stronger brains.

b Scientists are not sure why our memories are not always sharp.

c Good relationships are often more important for success at work than brain power.

d Blueberries, for example, have chemicals that help the brain.

e Wearing a bike helmet helps protect your head.

f Smoking has a negative effect on brain health.

g One way to prepare is to get enough sleep the night before the exam.

h One way is to use your computer mouse with the hand you wouldn't normally use.

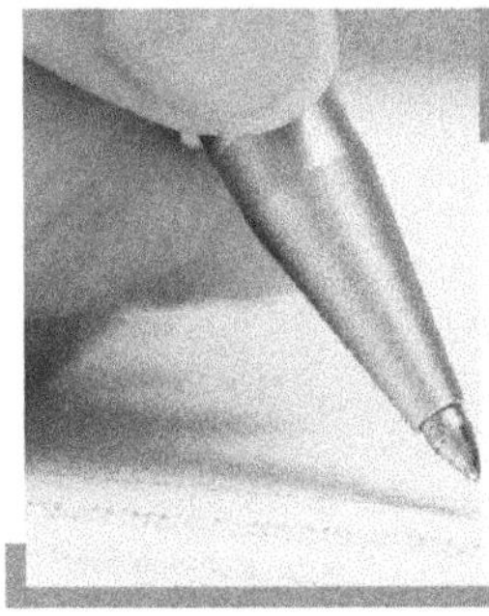

CHECK!

The key points to remember about a paragraph are:

- A paragraph has several sentences about ___________ topic.
- When you write, ___________ the first line of each paragraph.
- Only start a new ___________ when you start a new paragraph.
- Leave a ___________ between the period and the new sentence.

C. Practice

1 Check (✓) the paragraph in each pair that has the correct formatting.

1 ☐ **A** In the past, people believed that a person with a low IQ could not be successful.It's true that many people with high IQs are very successful in life.It's also true that many people with lower IQ scores have had very successful lives. Scientists continue to research whether IQ and success are connected.

☐ **B** In the past, people believed that a person with a low IQ could not be successful. It's true that many people with high IQs are very successful in life. It's also true that many people with lower IQ scores have had very successful lives. Scientists continue to research whether IQ and success are connected.

2 ☐ **A** What you eat affects your mental ability. We know that fish, nuts, berries, and whole grains are good for the body. Fatty fish and nuts contain chemicals that help the brain. Blueberries and whole grains are superfoods for the body and brain, too. Foods that are healthy for your body are also good for your brain.

☐ **B** What you eat affects your mental ability.
We know that fish, nuts, berries, and whole grains are good for the body.
Fatty fish and nuts contain chemicals that help the brain. Blueberries and whole grains are superfoods for the body and brain, too.
Foods that are healthy for your body are also good for your brain.

2 Read each paragraph. Check (✓) the two sentences that describe what is wrong.

1 Students should not stay up all night studying for tests.
First, it is difficult to get a good job if you do not go to school.
It is also hard to remember information before the exam.
Next, studying all night can make students feel sick and tired.
For these reasons, a healthy diet is good for physical health.

☐ a. The sentences are not all about the same topic.
☐ b. The first line is not indented.
☐ c. Each sentence is on a new line.
☐ d. There are no spaces between sentences.

2 Many people's brains become less sharp as they age.Older people are sharper in the morning.Younger people, on the other hand, think more quickly in the late afternoon. The afternoon can also be a good time to take a nap.

☐ a. The sentences are not all about the same topic.
☐ b. The first line is not indented.
☐ c. Each sentence is on a new line.
☐ d. There are no spaces between sentences.

D. Skill Quiz

Check (✓) the correct answer for each item.

1 A paragraph always has

- ☐ a. interesting information.
- ☐ b. sentences about the same topic.
- ☐ c. several main ideas.

2 Always indent the ___ line in a paragraph.

- ☐ a. first
- ☐ b. second
- ☐ c. last

3 Leave ___ spaces between a period and a new sentence.

- ☐ a. zero
- ☐ b. one or two
- ☐ c. about five

4 Choose the sentence that comes from the same paragraph as this main idea: *Some scientists think that worrying too much makes the brain weaker.*

- ☐ a. It is probably good to avoid stress if you want a strong brain.
- ☐ b. Many young people can think more quickly in the afternoon.
- ☐ c. Some successful people have high IQ scores.

5 Choose the sentence that comes from the same paragraph as this main idea: *Researchers say that mental exercise helps your brain power.*

- ☐ a. It is possible to feel happy and sad at the same time.
- ☐ b. There are many foods that improve brain health.
- ☐ c. Memory games and puzzles can help.

6 Choose the sentence that comes from the same paragraph as this main idea: *The brain causes people to feel emotions.*

- ☐ a. Staying up late does not help students do better on tests.
- ☐ b. The brain controls happiness and sadness.
- ☐ c. Not everyone thinks IQ scores are important for success.

7 *Students should not stay up all night studying for tests. First, it is difficult to get a good job if you do not go to school. It is also hard to remember information before the exam. Next, studying all night can make students feel sick and tired. For these reasons, a healthy diet is good for physical health.*

What is wrong with this paragraph?

- ☐ a. The first line is not indented.
- ☐ b. Not all sentences are from the same paragraph.
- ☐ c. The sentences are each on a new line.

8 *Happiness and sadness are connected to different parts of the brain.*
This is why people can feel both emotions at the same time.
When a child gets married, for example, a parent might feel happy and sad at the same time.
This information is helping doctors understand how to help people.

What is wrong with the formatting in this paragraph?

- ☐ a. The first line is not indented.
- ☐ b. There are no spaces after each sentence.
- ☐ c. The sentences are each on a new line.

3

Subject–Verb Agreement

WHAT'S APPROPRIATE?

Connecting to the Theme

How do you study best? Which sentence is most true for you?

A I like to study alone. **B** I learn best in a group. **C** I like to learn from a tutor.

Now think of last week. Think about how much time you spent studying alone, how much studying in a group with other students, and how much studying with a tutor. Did last week's studying match your preferred studying style?

A. Skill Presentation

When you write sentences, make sure the verb agrees with the subject. For example, the **subject** of this sentence is *Jerry*. The **verb** in this sentence is *greets*.

Jerry greets his professor.

Jerry is the singular subject. The singular verb is *greets*.

When the subject in a sentence has two or more nouns connected by *and*, use a plural verb.

Emma and her friend are working on a group project.

Emma and her friend is the plural subject, and the plural verb is *are working*.

When two or more singular subjects are connected by *or* or *nor*, use a singular verb. Use a singular verb because the verb agrees with either subject but not with both.

Tim or **Maria is** in my group.

Tim and *Maria* are the singular subjects. The singular verb is *is*.

B. Over to You

1 Read each sentence and decide if the verb should be singular or plural. Circle the correct verb.

1 Tony and Katerina *is* | *are* in Sara's study group.

2 Professor Espinoza or Professor Davis *e-mails* | *e-mail* assignments to the group.

3 Neither Rebecca nor George *is* | *are* in my group.

2 Complete the e-mail with the correct form of the verbs in parentheses.

To: Kate; Stephen; Ryoko; Tanya
Subject: First group meeting
From: Jim

Dear Kate, Stephen, Ryoko, and Tanya,

I am excited about our first group meeting this Wednesday. Stephen, Tanya, and I are going to meet at 8:00. Kate and Ryoko (have) [1]__________ class until 8:30. At the meeting, Tanya, Ryoko, and I (be) [2]__________ going to make a schedule. Kate or Ryoko is going to bring food. I think either Kate or Stephen (have) [3]__________ a copy of the assignment to share with everyone. Stephen and I have supplies, so we will bring paper and pens for everyone. However, neither his computer nor my computer (work) [4]__________. Tanya, can we use yours? Tanya, Ryoko, and Stephen (write) [5]__________ very well. Can one of you take notes at our meeting?

See you Wednesday!
Jim

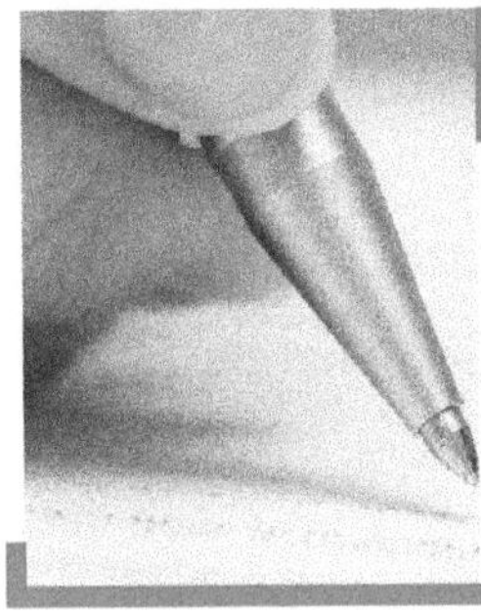

CHECK!

1 If your sentence has one subject, use a __________ verb.

2 If your sentence has more than one subject with *and*, use a __________ verb.

3 If your sentence has more than one subject with *or* or *nor*, use a __________ verb.

C. Practice

1 Read each sentence in the chart. Decide if the verb in bold is used correctly or not. Write *A*, *B* or *C*.

A This sentence is correct.
B Change the verb to a plural form.
C Change the verb to a singular form.

1. My professor and I **am** going to meet tomorrow.	
2. Either Isabel or Tam **are** going to send an e-mail to the group.	
3. Neither Chris nor Maya **has** my contact information.	
4. Rachel and I **are** in the same English class.	
5. Will and Louisa **is** not in the same English class.	
6. Neither Steve nor Vicky **are** in class today.	
7. Juan and Frieda **uses** abbreviations in their e-mails.	
8. Professor Chang and Professor Kim **prefers** brief e-mails.	
9. Mario and I **greets** each other in the morning.	
10. Neither Michael nor Carmen **is** in class today.	

2 Complete each sentence with the correct present simple form of the verb in parentheses.

1 Ryan and I ____________ in the same group. **(be)**
2 Neither Tom nor Selina ____________ ready for the meeting. **(be)**
3 Either Jon or Ana ____________ going to bring paper to the meeting. **(be)**
4 Amit and Vera ____________ with the group by e-mail. **(communicate)**
5 Amanda and Miki ____________ at 7 p.m. **(meet)**
6 Daniel and Julia ____________ Sissy. **(greet)**
7 Ron and Suzy ____________ their names and addresses on the contact sheet. **(write)**
8 Neither Fran nor Robert ____________ snacks to the meeting. **(bring)**
9 Either May or Andrew ____________ a schedule for the next meeting. **(make)**
10 Hans and Vito ____________ an e-mail to schedule the next meeting. **(send)**

D. Skill Quiz

Check (✓) the correct answer for each item.

1 When two or more singular subjects are connected by *or* or *nor*, use a

☐ a. singular verb.
☐ b. plural verb.
☐ c. plural subject.

2 When two or more singular subjects are connected by *and*, use a

☐ a. singular verb.
☐ b. plural verb.
☐ c. plural subject.

3 Choose the correct sentence.

☐ a. Tanya and I am making a schedule.
☐ b. Tanya and I are making a schedule.
☐ c. Tanya and I is making a schedule.

4 Choose the correct sentence.

☐ a. Either Yanni or Milena am bringing paper to the meeting.
☐ b. Either Yanni or Milena are bringing paper to the meeting.
☐ c. Either Yanni or Milena is bringing paper to the meeting.

5 Choose the correct sentence.

☐ a. Jenni and I are late for the meeting.
☐ b. Jenni and I is late for the meeting.
☐ c. Jenni and I am late for the meeting.

6 Choose the correct sentence.

☐ a. Miguel and Tam are in the same group.
☐ b. Miguel and Tam is meeting tomorrow.
☐ c. Miguel and Tam has good communication.

7 Choose the correct sentence.

☐ a. Kate and I writes the e-mail about last meeting.
☐ b. Kate and I send the e-mail about the next meeting.
☐ c. Kate and I opens the e-mails about the meeting.

8 Choose the correct sentence.

☐ a. Naim and Kay writes very polite e-mails.
☐ b. Naim and Kay greet each other politely.
☐ c. Naim and Kay uses polite language.

9 Choose the correct sentence.

☐ a. Neither Stefano nor Julie arrive at the meeting on time.
☐ b. Neither Stefano nor Julie knows where we are meeting.
☐ c. Neither Stefano nor Julie have copies of the schedule.

10 Choose the correct sentence.

☐ a. Riko and Francis bring snacks to the meeting.
☐ b. Riko and Francis eats snacks at the meeting.
☐ c. Riko and Francis makes snacks for the meeting.

4

Capitalization Rules 1

ENTREPRENEURS

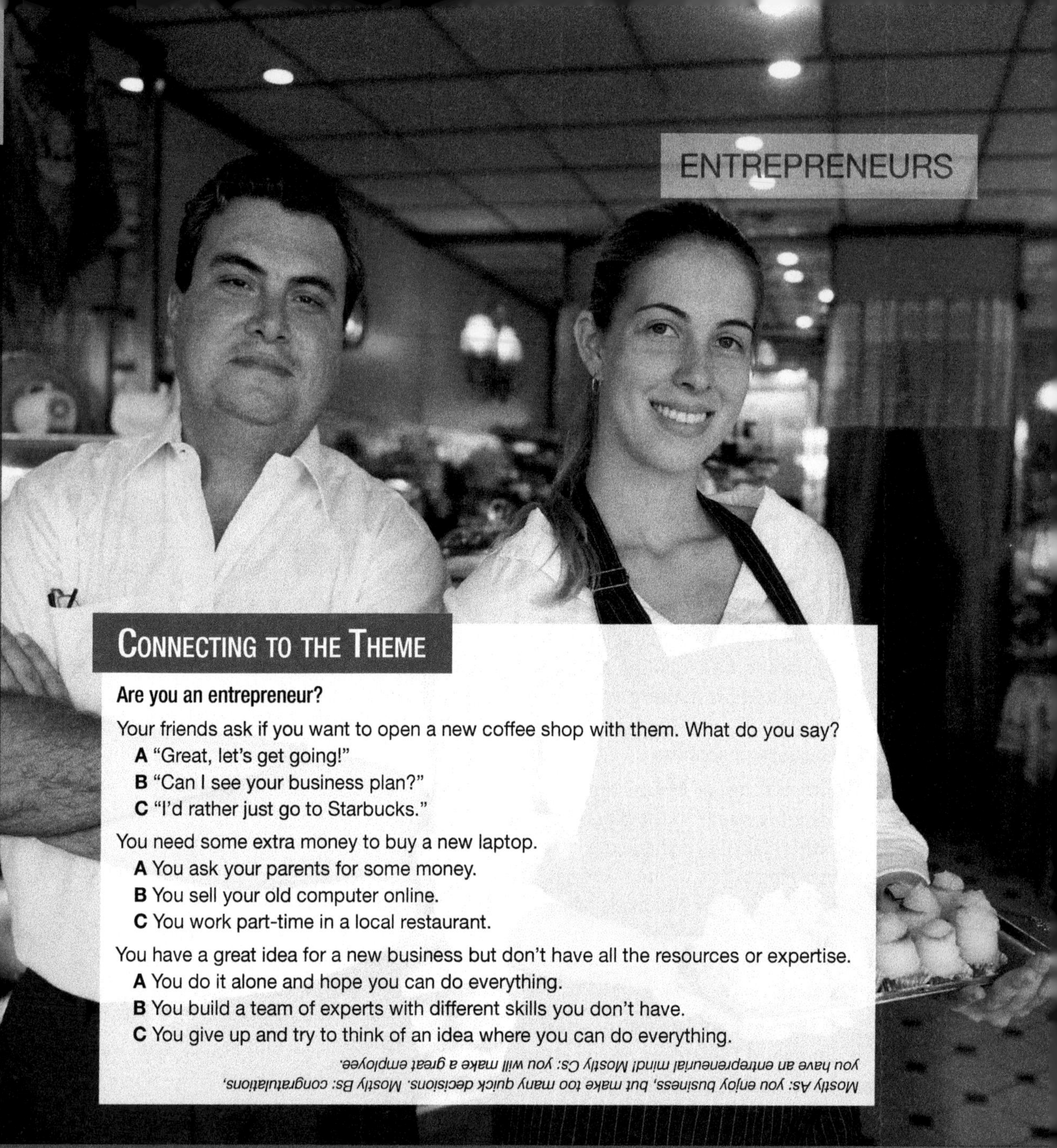

Connecting to the Theme

Are you an entrepreneur?

Your friends ask if you want to open a new coffee shop with them. What do you say?

A "Great, let's get going!"
B "Can I see your business plan?"
C "I'd rather just go to Starbucks."

You need some extra money to buy a new laptop.

A You ask your parents for some money.
B You sell your old computer online.
C You work part-time in a local restaurant.

You have a great idea for a new business but don't have all the resources or expertise.

A You do it alone and hope you can do everything.
B You build a team of experts with different skills you don't have.
C You give up and try to think of an idea where you can do everything.

Mostly As: you enjoy business, but make too many quick decisions. Mostly Bs: congratulations, you have an entrepreneurial mind! Mostly Cs: you will make a great employee.

A. Skill Presentation

In English, it's important to know when to **capitalize.** To capitalize a letter is to make it a capital. Capital letters are usually bigger than lowercase letters.

Let's look at some rules for using capital letters.

- Always capitalize the first letter of the first word in a sentence.
- Always capitalize the pronoun *I*.
- Always capitalize the first letter of the names of specific people, places, businesses, and organizations. We call these specific things **proper nouns**.
- Always capitalize the first letter of cities, countries, and nationalities. These are proper nouns, too.

B. Over to You

1 Read the sentences. Circle any letters that should be capitalized.

1 students place orders online. employees deliver the orders on bicycles.

2 i started my own business. i design websites, and i work from home.

3 One of the cofounders of google is sergey brin. He went to stanford university.

4 I went to beijing for work last year. I helped a chinese company train new employees. I enjoyed working in china.

2 Read the e-mail below. Decide if the letters in parentheses should be capital or not. Write capital or lowercase letters in the space provided.

To: Jennifer
Subject: New business idea
From: Sam

1 Hi [a](j) ___ennifer,

[b](i) ___ had a great [c](i) ___dea for a new [d](b) ___usiness.

2 [a](i) ___ thought you might be interested in my [b](i) ___dea.

3 I was reading in the [a](n) ___ew [b](y) ___ork [c](t) ___imes that it's a great time to start a [d](b) ___usiness.

4 [a](m) ___y friends always complain that they have no help when their [b](p) ___ersonal [c](c) ___omputers are broken.

5 [a](i) ___ think [b](a) ___llentown really needs a [c](c) ___ompany that provides [d](t) ___echnology support.

6 [a](w) ___e could hire [b](e) ___mployees to visit people's homes and fix their [c](c) ___omputers.

7 [a](w) ___e could rent that [b](o) ___ffice above the [c](j) ___ade [d](g) ___arden restaurant.

8 [a](l) ___et me know if [b](y) ___ou'd like to take advantage of this opportunity!

[c](s) ___am.

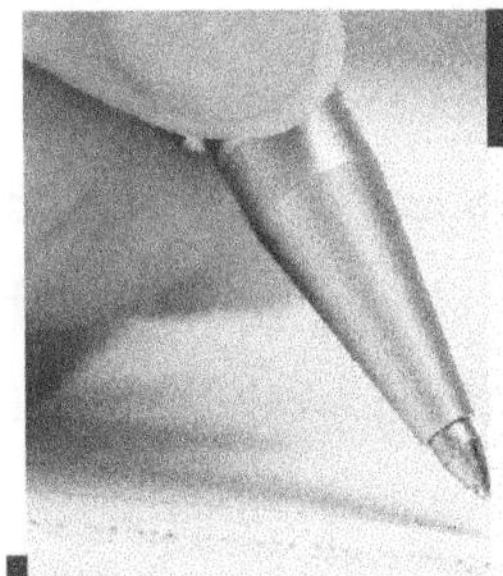

CHECK!

1 Capitalize the ___________ word in a sentence.

2 Capitalize the ___________ *I*.

3 Capitalize ___________ nouns. These include specific people, ___________, businesses, and organizations as well as cities, countries, and ___________.

C. Practice

1 Read the sentences and check (✓) the words that should be capitalized.

1 at yale university, business student seth goldman loved to exercise. Unfortunately, he couldn't find anything good to drink after his workout. In time, he created his own drink.

- ☐ a. at, yale university, seth goldman
- ☐ b. business student, he, his
- ☐ c. loved, find, drink

2 seth's professor, barry nalebuff, helped market the drink. They named their product honest tea.

- ☐ a. seth's, barry nalebuff, honest tea
- ☐ b. helped, named, their
- ☐ c. professor, drink, product

3 Seth took Honest tea to a famous supermarket company. the supermarket ordered 15,000 bottles from seth!

- ☐ a. famous, supermarket, company
- ☐ b. tea, the, seth
- ☐ c. took, ordered, bottles

4 The tea that Seth and barry created was an immediate success thanks to their hard work. now they produce 20 varieties of healthy tea and juice drinks.

- ☐ a. tea, their
- ☐ b. healthy, juice
- ☐ c. barry, now

5 Even president barack Obama asked for bottles of his favorite Honest Tea drinks to be kept at the White house in case he got thirsty.

- ☐ a. president, barack, house
- ☐ b. bottles, drinks, thirsty
- ☐ c. the, his, he

2 Read the sentences. Circle the correct form of the words.

1 *my* | *My* laptop will not work.

2 A *friend* | *Friend* said that I might have to buy a new one.

3 I just returned from a trip to *South America* | *south America* to expand my business there.

4 My laptop worked fine when I met with new clients in *lima, Peru* | *Lima, Peru.*

5 At my meetings in Argentina and Chile, *it* | *It* wouldn't work.

6 I asked a *Brazilian Friend* | *Brazilian friend* to try to fix it, but he made it worse.

7 I was hoping it would work at *John F. Kennedy* | *John f. Kennedy* Airport, but it didn't.

8 I'm home in *New York City* | *New york city* now, and I can't run my business without it.

9 I contacted a *computer repair company* | *Computer Repair Company* called Millenium Tech.

10 I might have to go to their store on *Spring street* | *Spring Street* to get it fixed.

D. Skill Quiz

Check (✓) the correct answer for each item.

1 Which pronoun is always capitalized?

☐ a. I
☐ b. You
☐ c. They

2 Capitalize ___ word in a sentence.

☐ a. the first
☐ b. the last
☐ c. every

3 Always capitalize ___.

☐ a. nouns
☐ b. seasons
☐ c. countries

4 The word ___ is a proper noun, so it should be capitalized.

☐ a. Company
☐ b. Chicago
☐ c. e-mail

5 Choose the lowercase word that should be capitalized in this sentence: *as a young man, Matthew Mandell was interested in business.*

☐ a. as
☐ b. man
☐ c. business

6 Choose the lowercase word that should be capitalized in this sentence: *Later, Matthew went to college in washington, D.C.*

☐ a. college
☐ b. in
☐ c. washington

7 Choose the lowercase word that should be capitalized in this sentence: *Seth goldman created Honest Tea because he was thirsty.*

☐ a. goldman
☐ b. because
☐ c. thirsty

8 Choose the lowercase word that should be capitalized in this sentence: *The company makes the tea in maryland and ships it all over the United States.*

☐ a. company
☐ b. maryland
☐ c. it

9 Choose the lowercase word that should be capitalized in this sentence: *My family lives in Seattle, and i work at Microsoft.*

☐ a. family
☐ b. in
☐ c. i

10 Choose the lowercase word that should be capitalized in this sentence: *i want to start my own graphic design company in New York.*

☐ a. i
☐ b. graphic
☐ c. design

5

Punctuation 1: Periods, Question Marks, and Commas in Lists

SCIENCE AND SOCIETY

Connecting to the Theme

Test your knowledge!

A vaccine is a medicine that protects people from getting diseases. Which of these diseases is there a vaccine for?

- smallpox
- influenza
- AIDS
- polio
- common cold
- malaria
- measles
- cancer

Answers: There are vaccines for smallpox, influenza, polio, and measles.

A. Skill Presentation

We use punctuation to end sentences. There are different ways to end sentences.

If the sentence is a statement, end it with a **period**.

Dr. Hilleman is a famous scientist.

If the sentence is a question, end it with a **question mark**.

Is Dr. Hilleman a famous scientist?

Use punctuation to separate items in a list. Use **commas** to do this. When you are only listing two items with *and*, do not use a comma.

Dr. Khan studies diseases and vaccines.

When you are listing three or more items, you need to use commas. Put a comma after each item except for the last item.

Cynthia is taking chemistry, history, and public health.

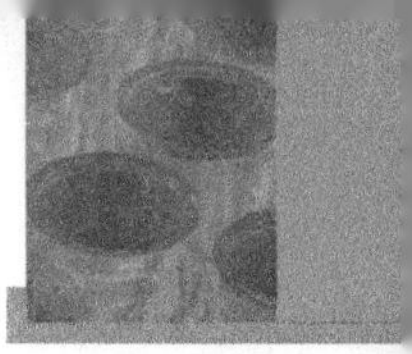

B. Over to You

1 How should you end these sentences? Circle the correct punctuation.

1 Do chemists try to find cures for diseases . | ?

2 Dr. Bayley discovered a new medicine . | ?

2 Where do the commas go in these sentences? Add commas in the correct places. If no comma is needed, leave it blank.

1 Chad hopes to study medicine and ancient societies.

2 Elena has to get vaccinations for the flu chicken pox and polio.

3 Look at the punctuation (periods, question marks, and commas) in each sentence in the chart. Decide if it is correct or incorrect, and check (✓) the box in the correct column.

	CORRECT PUNCTUATION	INCORRECT PUNCTUATION
1. Chemists try to find cures for diseases?		
2. Common vaccines are flu, measles and diphtheria.		
3. Many babies, children, and adults get vaccines every year.		
4. Did you get a vaccine last year?		
5. When was your last vaccine.		
6. I got two vaccines last year?		
7. Flu, and diphtheria are common vaccines.		
8. Dr. Behring and Dr. Hilleman are famous doctors.		
9. Does your school require vaccination.		
10. The doctor told Maria to get a vaccine.		

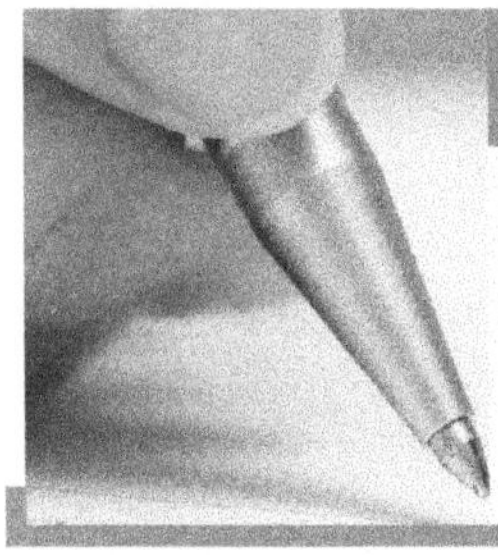

CHECK!

1 End a statement with a ____________.

2 End a question with a ____________.

3 In a list of two items, do not use a ____________.

4 In a list of three or more items, use a ____________.

C. Practice

1 Read the statements and questions. Put a question mark or a period at the end of each sentence.

1 Are vaccines important discoveries ___
2 Did Dr. Behring discover a vaccine ___
3 Many people get vaccines ___
4 Which chemist discovered the measles vaccine ___
5 For some people, gym memberships are luxuries ___
6 Modern medicine includes many different vaccines ___
7 People did not have vaccines in ancient times ___
8 Was Karen's flu vaccine on her medical record ___
9 How many flu vaccines are available ___
10 Vaccines have had a big effect on public health ___

2 Read the sentences and add commas where necessary. If no comma is needed, leave it blank.

1 Most babies children and adults in the United States are vaccinated.
2 Common vaccines are chicken pox measles and the flu.
3 Measles and flu are newer vaccines.
4 Young children and older adults should get flu vaccines.
5 Dr. Behring and Dr. Hilleman discovered vaccines.
6 Common effects from the flu are fever cough and headache.
7 Children in Germany France and Canada get vaccines.
8 Chicken pox measles and flu vaccines did not exist in ancient times.
9 I looked at my paper record and my online record of vaccines.
10 Positive effects of vaccines are better health and a longer life.

D. Skill Quiz

Check (✓) the correct answer for each item.

1 A statement ends with a

☐ a. comma.
☐ b. period.
☐ c. question mark.

2 A sentence that starts with *Why* and a form of *be* ends with a

☐ a. comma.
☐ b. period.
☐ c. question mark.

3 In a list of two items, use ___ comma(s).

☐ a. no
☐ b. one
☐ c. two

4 In a list of three items, use a comma ___ the word *and*.

☐ a. after
☐ b. before
☐ c. instead of

5 Which list shows the correct use of commas?

☐ a. chicken pox, measles and flu
☐ b. chicken pox, measles, and, flu
☐ c. chicken pox, measles, and flu

6 *Medicine is important for disease prevention, and health.*
This sentence is incorrect because

☐ a. there should not be a comma after prevention.
☐ b. there should be a question mark, not a period.
☐ c. there should be another comma after and.

7 *Dr. Garret studied medicine in Japan India and Norway.*
This sentence is incorrect because

☐ a. there should be a comma after and.
☐ b. there should be commas after Japan and India.
☐ c. there should be a question mark, not a period.

8 Which sentence is correct?

☐ a. Did you look at your medical record.
☐ b. You looked at your medical record?
☐ c. When did you look at your medical record?

9 Which sentence is correct?

☐ a. Dr. Hilleman discovered a vaccine?
☐ b. What vaccine did Dr. Hilleman discover?
☐ c. What vaccine did Dr. Hilleman discover.

10 Choose the correct punctuation to end this sentence: *When was the first vaccine discovered* ___

☐ a. !
☐ b. .
☐ c. ?

6 Consistent Pronoun Use

MEMORABLE EVENTS

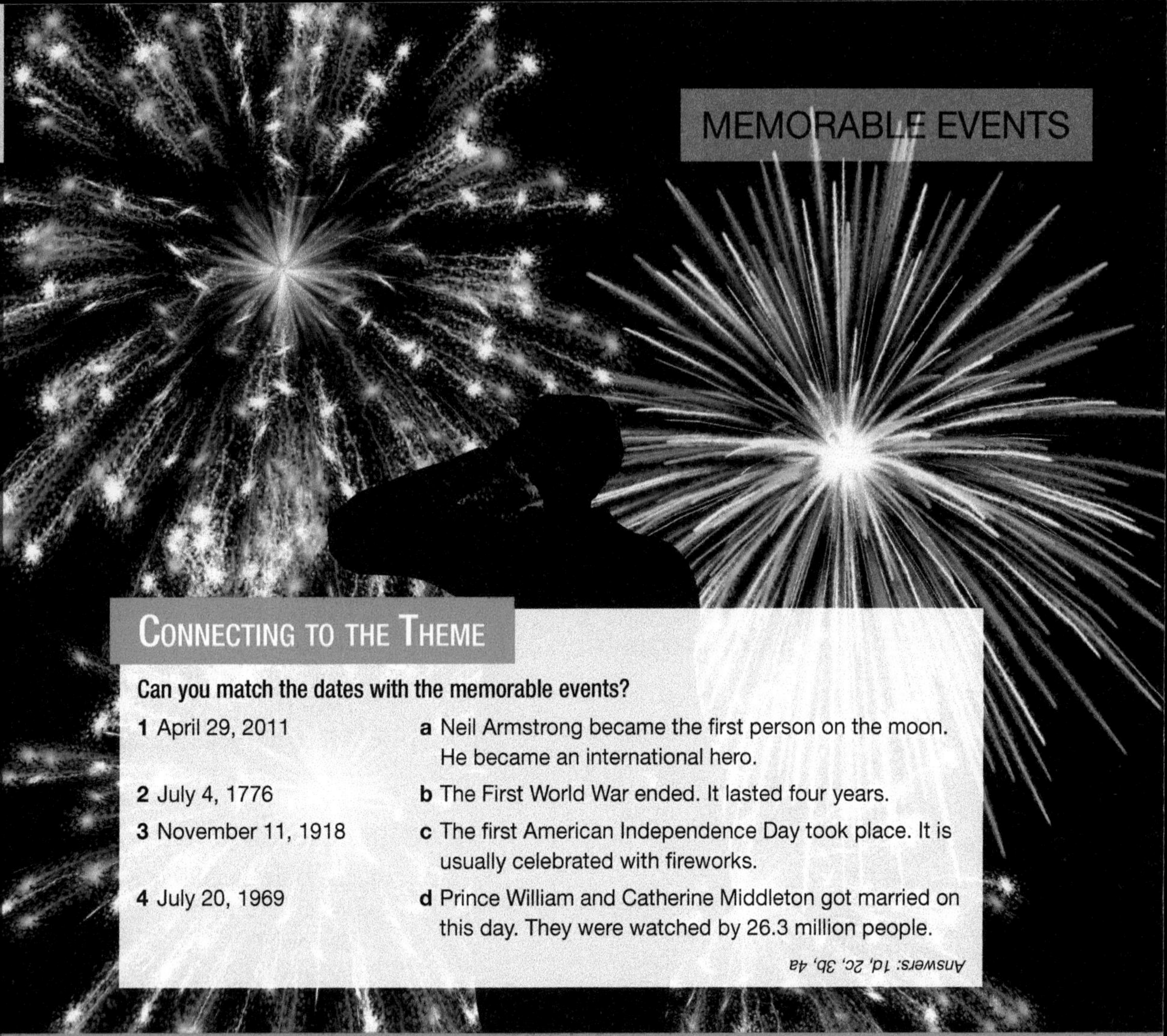

Connecting to the Theme

Can you match the dates with the memorable events?

1 April 29, 2011	**a** Neil Armstrong became the first person on the moon. He became an international hero.
2 July 4, 1776	**b** The First World War ended. It lasted four years.
3 November 11, 1918	**c** The first American Independence Day took place. It is usually celebrated with fireworks.
4 July 20, 1969	**d** Prince William and Catherine Middleton got married on this day. They were watched by 26.3 million people.

Answers: 1d, 2c, 3b, 4a

A. Skill Presentation

Pronouns are words that are used in place of nouns. **Subject pronouns** are used for nouns that are **subjects.** *I*, *you*, *he*, *she*, *it*, *we*, and *they* are subject pronouns.

It's important to use the correct pronouns when you write.

> **Sixty-two thousand people** attended the ceremony. **They** saw many memorable images.

Sixty-two thousand people is the subject of this sentence. In the second sentence, the pronoun *they* replaces *sixty-two thousand people.*

> **The opening ceremony** was wonderful. **It** was attended by sixty-two thousand people.

If there is more than one noun, be sure you use the pronoun for the correct noun. In the second sentence, the pronoun *it* replaces the subject *the opening ceremony*.

When you write, remember to replace a noun with the same pronoun every time. This is called using pronouns consistently.

> Thousands of people were in the ceremony. **They** wore beautiful clothes, and **they** created many memorable moments.

In the first sentence, *Thousands of people* is the subject. Use *they* every time you replace *thousands of people* with a pronoun.

B. Over to You

1 Which subject pronouns replace the words in bold? Circle the correct pronouns.

1 **My friend and I** watched the ceremony on TV. *You* | *We* thought it was memorable, too. *You* | *We* will never forget those images.

2 **More than 7 million people** watched Felix Baumgartner jump from the edge of space. *He* | *They* watched him online on their computers, tablets, and phones.

2 Choose the correct pronoun to complete each sentence.

I he she it we you they

1 Tom and I will always remember the London opening ceremony. We didn't go, but we saw it on TV. ______ was very impressive!

2 My sister really enjoyed the closing ceremony. ______ liked the music best.

3 The International Olympic Committee chooses where the Olympic games will be held. ______ votes on which city would make the best location.

4 My friends and I really enjoy watching soccer. We think soccer is the best event in the Olympics, and ______ watch it as often as possible.

5 Ken and Mia went to an Olympic hockey game. I couldn't go because ______ couldn't get a ticket.

6 The lights at the opening ceremony were bright, and ______ were truly amazing.

7 Donna attended the 2010 Winter Olympics in Vancouver, Canada. She took lots of pictures, and ______ shared them online.

8 Why couldn't Clive compete in the Olympics? Was ______ hurt?

9 The power failed in our house, and all the lights went out. ______ were out for five hours, and we missed the opening ceremony.

10 You can watch the whole opening ceremony online, if ______ missed it.

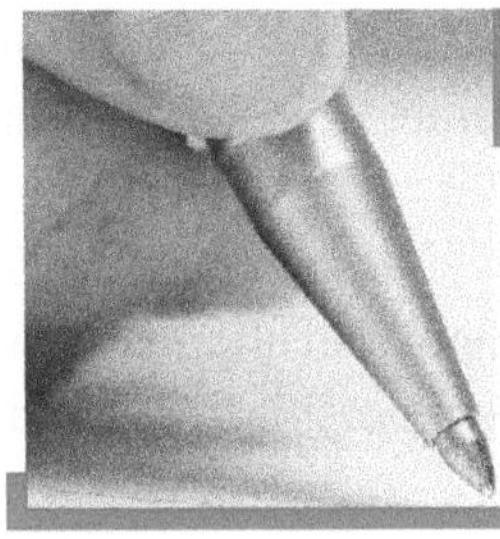

CHECK!

1 Always use pronouns correctly and consistently to replace ____________.

2 Subject pronouns are used in place of nouns that are ____________.

3 *I*, *you*, ____________, *she*, *it*, ____________, ____________, and *they* are subject pronouns.

C. Practice

1 Read the paragraph. Circle the numbered subject pronouns that refer to "a solar eclipse."

What is a solar eclipse?

A solar eclipse is when the moon blocks the light of the sun. There are partial solar eclipses and total solar eclipses. In a total eclipse, you cannot see any of the sun's light because [1]it is completely blocked by the moon. A solar eclipse usually only lasts a few minutes. Experts say the longest [2]it can last is seven and a half minutes. A very long solar eclipse happened on July 22, 2009. [3]It lasted 6 minutes and 39 seconds. Experts say [4]it was very rare. [5]They say a longer eclipse won't happen until June 13, 2132.

2 Match each sentence (1–5) with the correct supporting sentence (a–e).

___ **1** Mark saw the solar eclipse in 2009.

___ **2** Victoria also saw the eclipse.

___ **3** A partial solar eclipse happened on January 15, 2010.

___ **4** More solar eclipses will happen in the next decade.

___ **5** Mark, Victoria, and I plan to see the next solar eclipse.

a They can be predicted using computer systems.

b He said it was very memorable.

c It lasted more than 11 minutes, and it made the sky much darker.

d We will look at it with special glasses.

e She will never forget the image in the sky.

3 Read the paragraph and circle the correct pronouns.

The 2012 Summer Olympics

The 2012 Summer Olympics were held in London, England. The opening ceremony was a wonderful celebration. Exactly 15,000 people took part in it. [1]*It* | *They* were very lucky to be chosen. Nearly 1 billion people watched the show on television. [2]*It* | *They* was one of the most popular opening ceremonies ever. Danny Boyle directed it. [3]*It* | *He* is a movie director, so the ceremony had a lot of actors in it. Kenneth Branagh is a famous actor. [4]*He* | *They* read a piece of Shakespeare. The famous soccer player David Beckham had an important role, too. [5]*It* | *He* brought the Olympic torch to the stadium in a speed boat! Lots of children also participated. [6]*We* | *They* will always remember taking part.

D. Skill Quiz

Check (✓) the correct answer for each item.

1 Words that are used in place of nouns are called

- ☐ a. pronouns.
- ☐ b. prepositions.
- ☐ c. verbs.

2 Replacing a subject with the same pronoun every time is called using the pronoun

- ☐ a. consistently.
- ☐ b. differently.
- ☐ c. incorrectly.

3 Choose the correct subject pronouns to complete the sentences: *Neil Armstrong walked on the moon in 1969. ___ was the first man to do it, and ___ became famous.*

- ☐ a. He, he
- ☐ b. It, he
- ☐ c. He, they

4 Choose the correct subject pronouns to complete the sentences: *There was a total solar eclipse on July 20, 1963. ___ lasted about a minute. ___ was the shortest total solar eclipse of the century.*

- ☐ a. They, it
- ☐ b. It, It
- ☐ c. It, they

5 Choose the correct subject pronoun to complete the sentence: *The Olympics opening ceremony was on February 12, and ___ was amazing.*

- ☐ a. it
- ☐ b. they
- ☐ c. she

6 Choose the correct subject pronouns to complete the sentences: *Paul went to a concert last night. ___ said the concert was amazing. ___ was three hours long.*

- ☐ a. He, They
- ☐ b. He, It
- ☐ c. He, He

7 Choose the correct subject pronouns to complete the sentences: *That website listed the ten most memorable events of the decade. ___ said that Hurricane Katrina was one of them. ___ also listed memorable events for other decades.*

- ☐ a. It, They
- ☐ b. They, We
- ☐ c. It, It

8 Choose the correct subject pronouns to complete the sentences: *I remember when the power failed. ___ happened in the summer. Julia couldn't get home because the subway system shut down. ___ slept at her office.*

- ☐ a. It, She
- ☐ b. She, They
- ☐ c. It, They

9 Choose the subject pronouns to complete the sentences: *Sandra and I don't usually go to a party on New Year's Eve. However, ___ went to a huge celebration for the millennium. ___ was incredible.*

- ☐ a. they, It
- ☐ b. we, They
- ☐ c. we, It

10 Choose the subject pronouns to complete the sentences: *Do you remember the Y2K bug? People were very worried ___ would damage lots of computers. In the end, ___ were wrong. ___ did not damage many computers.*

- ☐ a. it, they, It
- ☐ b. they, they, They
- ☐ c. she, it, it

7

Avoiding Run-Ons and Comma Splices

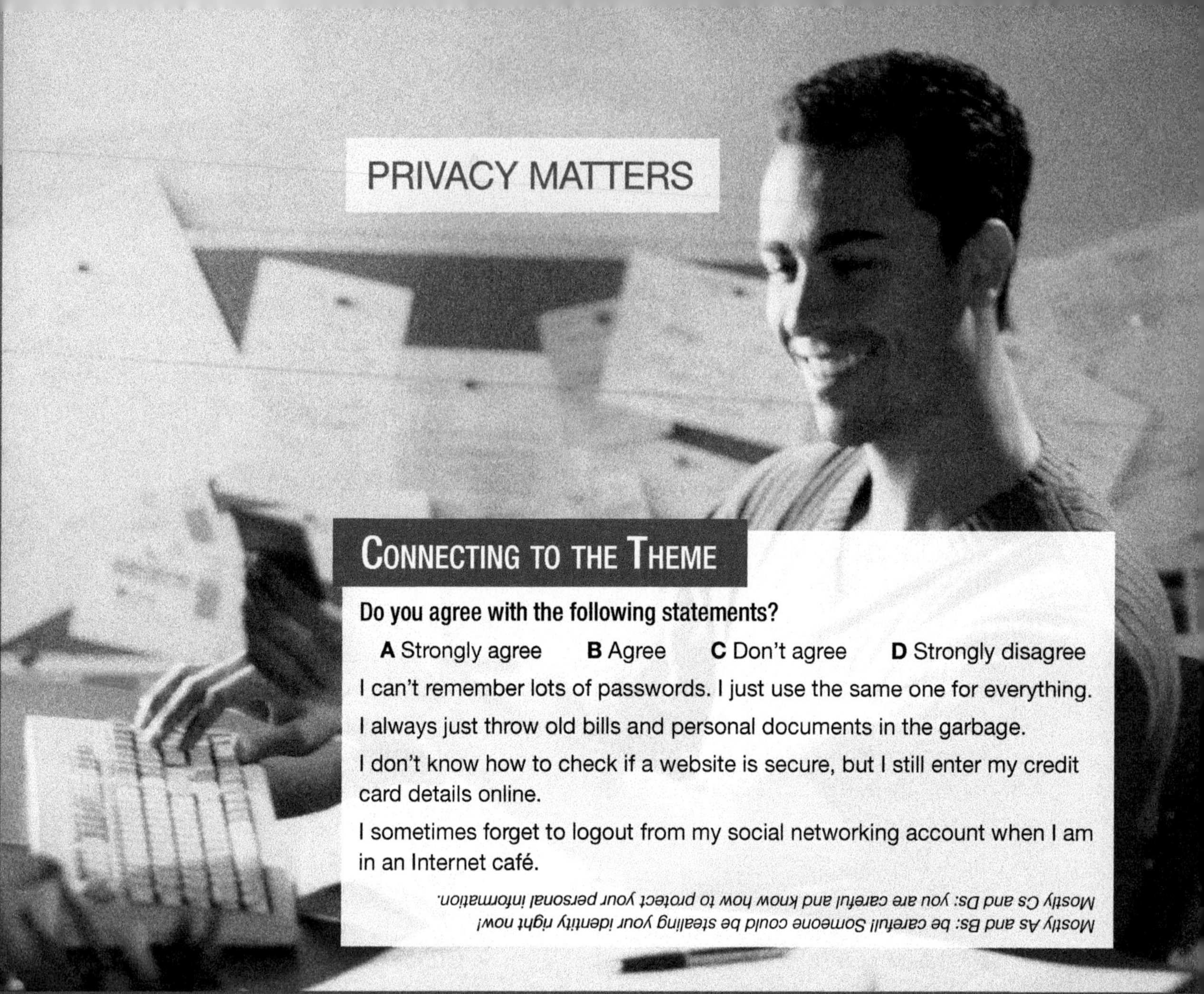

PRIVACY MATTERS

Connecting to the Theme

Do you agree with the following statements?

A Strongly agree **B** Agree **C** Don't agree **D** Strongly disagree

I can't remember lots of passwords. I just use the same one for everything.

I always just throw old bills and personal documents in the garbage.

I don't know how to check if a website is secure, but I still enter my credit card details online.

I sometimes forget to logout from my social networking account when I am in an Internet café.

Mostly As and Bs: be careful! Someone could be stealing your identity right now!

Mostly Cs and Ds: you are careful and know how to protect your personal information.

A. Skill Presentation

An independent clause has a subject and a verb, and it expresses a complete idea. A **run-on sentence** has two or more independent clauses that are joined without a comma or a conjunction. They are grammatically incorrect in English, so avoid them when you write.

— INDEPENDENT CLAUSE 1 — ——— INDEPENDENT CLAUSE 2 ———

Hannah protects her privacy she does not share personal information. ✗

A **comma splice** is similar to a run-on sentence. It is when two or more independent clauses are connected only by a comma. There is no conjunction.

—— INDEPENDENT CLAUSE 1 —— ——— INDEPENDENT CLAUSE 2 ———

Hannah worries about identity theft, she creates passwords for her accounts. ✗

Comma splices are also grammatically incorrect in English, so avoid them when you write.

Here are two ways to avoid run-on sentences and comma splices.

1 Make two sentences.

Hannah protects her privacy. **She** does not share personal information.

2 Add a conjunction between the independent clauses. For example, you can add *and*, *but*, *or*, *nor*, or *so*. Remember to use a comma, too.

Hannah protects her privacy, **so** she does not share personal information.

B. Over to You

1 Rewrite the run-on sentence by making two sentences or by adding a conjunction.

Hannah shops on secure websites she uses good passwords.

____

2 Read the sentences and write *C* for Correct, *RO* for Run-On, or *CS* for Comma Splice.

1 ___ a. Identity theft is a problem in the United States. You can prevent it by protecting your personal information.
___ b. Identity theft is a problem in the United States you can prevent it by protecting your personal information.

2 ___ a. Jorge got an e-mail from a stranger he did not reply to it.
___ b. Jorge got an e-mail from a stranger, so he did not reply to it.

3 ___ a. You should destroy old documents, you should also keep your passport safe.
___ b. You should destroy old documents. You should also keep your passport safe.

4 ___ a. Daniel has good passwords for his accounts. He is careful when he is online.
___ b. Daniel has good passwords for his accounts he is careful when he is online.

5 ___ a. You can keep important documents in a safe place, or you can destroy them.
___ b. You can keep important documents in a safe place, you can destroy them.

6 ___ a. Maya wants to choose a good password I told her not to use her birthday.
___ b. Maya wants to choose a good password, so I told her not to use her birthday.

7 ___ a. Alejandro worried about identity theft, but he did not do anything to avoid it.
___ b. Alejandro worried about identity theft, he did not do anything to avoid it.

8 ___ a. It is a good idea to shop on secure websites, you should never tell anyone your password.
___ b. It is a good idea to shop on secure websites, and you should never tell anyone your password.

9 ___ a. Tomas uses the same passwords for all of his accounts he should change them.
___ b. Tomas uses the same passwords for all of his accounts. He should change them.

10 ___ a. Ana's credit cards were stolen, so she had to get new ones.
___ b. Ana's credit cards were stolen she had to get new ones.

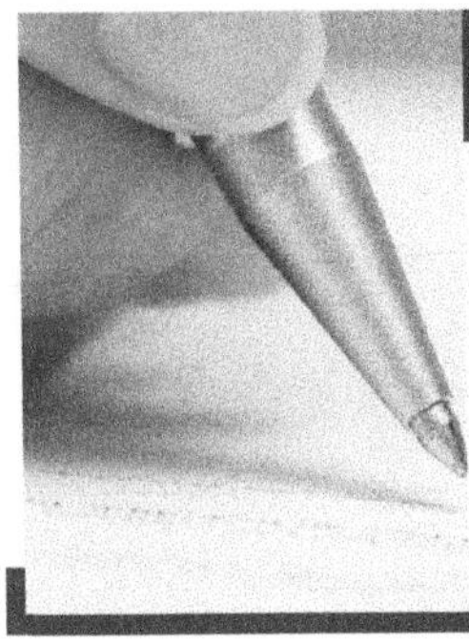

CHECK!

1 A ___________ ___________ has two or more independent clauses joined without a comma or a conjunction.

2 A ___________ ___________ is when two or more independent clauses are connected only by a comma. There is no conjunction.

3 Avoid run-on sentences and comma splices when you write. Make ___________ sentences, or use a comma with a ___________.

C. Practice

1 Read each sentence in the chart and decide if it is a correct sentence, a run-on sentence, or a comma splice. Check (✓) the box in the correct column.

	RUN-ON SENTENCE	COMMA SPLICE	CORRECT
1. Jin was a victim of identity theft, and her personal information was stolen.			
2. Now Jin shops on secure websites she uses strong passwords for her bank accounts.			
3. Karin wants to protect her identity, she only goes on safe websites.			
4. Karin could cut up the documents, or she could buy a shredder.			
5. I don't reply to e-mails from strangers I also don't shop on unsecure websites.			
6. I received a message from a stranger in my e-mail, I did not reply to it.			
7. My friend Jorge wants to protect his identity, he always leaves his passport at home.			
8. Jorge loves to shop for clothes online he only shops on secure websites.			
9. All of Maya's passwords are the same she should change them.			
10. Maya is worried about choosing good passwords, so I told her to pick something no one could guess.			

2 Read these tips for good passwords, and check (✓) the run-on sentences. Rewrite them correctly below.

- ☐ Your password should be at least six letters long.
- ☐ Good passwords have uppercase and lowercase letters it is good to include both.
- ☐ Your password should be easy to remember it should be difficult for other people to guess.
- ☐ Use different passwords for all of your accounts.
- ☐ You should keep your passwords private. Don't share them with anyone don't write them down.

1 ____

2 ____

3 ____

D. Skill Quiz

Check (✓) the correct answer for each item.

1 Which choice describes an independent clause?

☐ a. It has a subject, and it expresses an incomplete idea.
☐ b. It has two subjects and no verb.
☐ c. It has a subject and a verb, and it expresses a complete idea.

2 What is usually missing in a comma splice?

☐ a. a comma
☐ b. a complete idea
☐ c. a conjunction

3 What is one way to fix a run-on sentence?

☐ a. Add a period to make two sentences.
☐ b. Add a comma, but do not add a conjunction.
☐ c. Add a subject and a verb.

4 Choose the run-on sentence.

☐ a. Joe was a victim of identity theft. He protects his personal information carefully now.
☐ b. Joe was a victim of identity theft, he protects his personal information carefully now.
☐ c. Joe was a victim of identity theft he protects his personal information carefully now.

5 Choose the run-on sentence.

☐ a. Alejandro always leaves his passport at home, he only needs it when he travels.
☐ b. Alejandro always leaves his passport at home he only needs it when he travels.
☐ c. Alejandro always leaves his passport at home. He only needs it when he travels.

6 Choose the comma splice.

☐ a. Hana was a victim of identity theft it made it difficult for her to get loans.
☐ b. Hana was a victim of identity theft, so it made it difficult for her to get loans.
☐ c. Hana was a victim of identity theft, it made it difficult for her to get loans.

7 Choose the option that is not a run-on or a comma splice.

☐ a. Mateo could delete personal information he could keep it in a secure place.
☐ b. Mateo could delete personal information, or he could keep it in a secure place.
☐ c. Mateo could delete personal information, he could keep it in a secure place.

8 Choose the option that is not a run-on or a comma splice.

☐ a. I received an e-mail from a stranger I didn't reply to it.
☐ b. I received an e-mail from a stranger. I didn't reply to it.
☐ c. I received an e-mail from a stranger, I didn't reply to it.

8

Avoiding Sentence Fragments

THE MEDIA

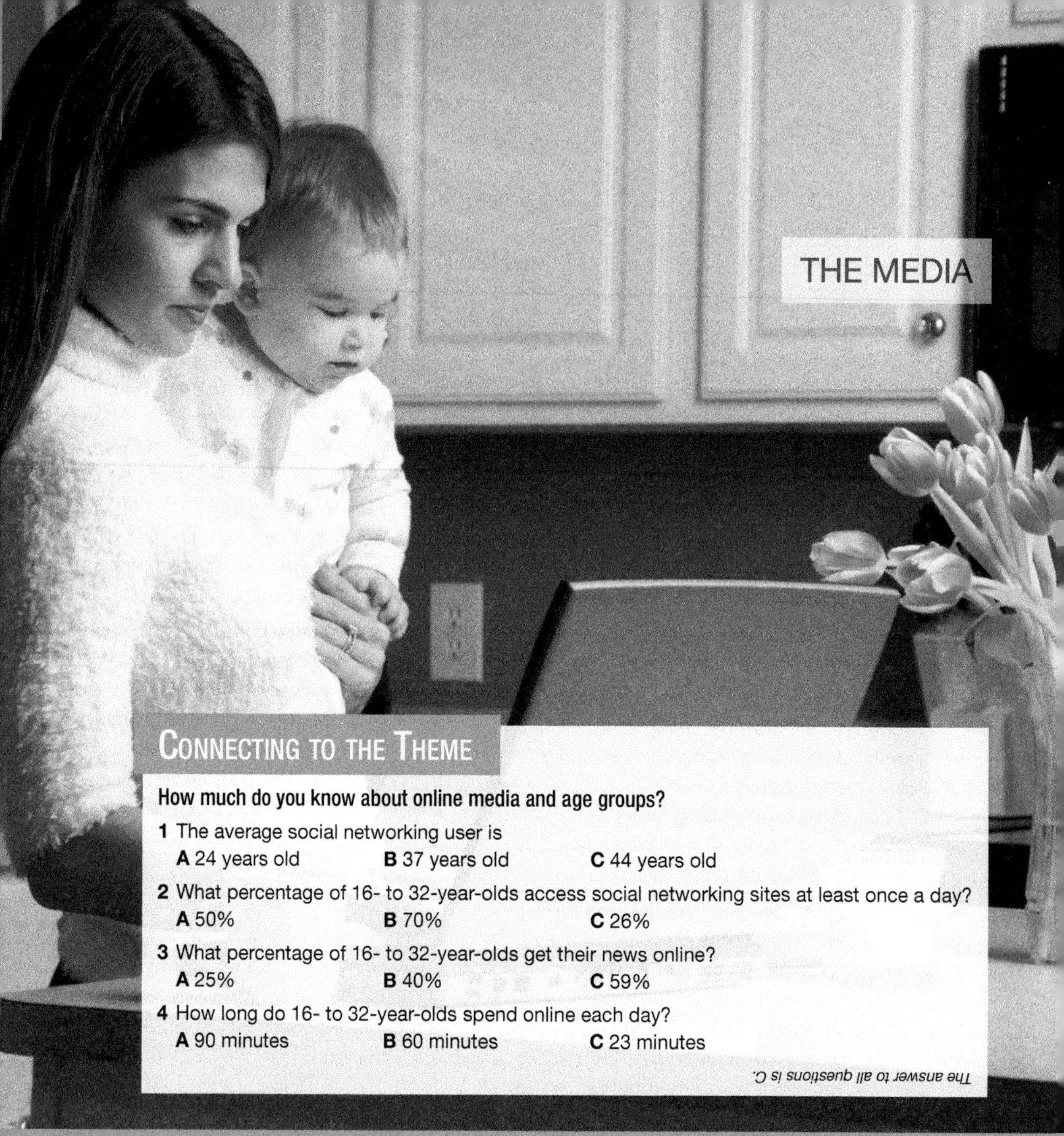

Connecting to the Theme

How much do you know about online media and age groups?

1 The average social networking user is
A 24 years old **B** 37 years old **C** 44 years old

2 What percentage of 16- to 32-year-olds access social networking sites at least once a day?
A 50% **B** 70% **C** 26%

3 What percentage of 16- to 32-year-olds get their news online?
A 25% **B** 40% **C** 59%

4 How long do 16- to 32-year-olds spend online each day?
A 90 minutes **B** 60 minutes **C** 23 minutes

The answer to all questions is C.

A. Skill Presentation

A complete sentence in English has a **subject** and a **verb**, and it expresses a complete idea.

Social networking sites are a great way to connect with friends and family.

It is important to avoid sentence fragments in your writing. Sentence fragments are sentences that do not contain a subject or a verb and do not express a complete idea.

Remember that some verbs need an auxiliary verb – either *be* (*am, is, are*) or *do* (*do, does*).

Is writing comments. ✗ (the subject is missing)

She writing comments. ✗ (the auxiliary verb *is* is missing)

She is writing comments. ✓

B. Over to You

1 Read the paragraph and correct the sentences by adding a verb or subject where necessary.

Social networking sites [1]__________ not just for young people. Everyone uses them. They are a great way to connect with friends and family. However, [2]__________ should pay close attention to proper social networking rules.

2 Read the sentence fragments and decide if the subject or the verb is missing. Check (✓) the correct answer.

1 Social networking sites used by people of all ages.
- ☐ subject missing
- ☐ verb missing

2 However, must not forget the etiquette of social networking.
- ☐ subject missing
- ☐ verb missing

3 Read each item in the chart, and decide if it is a complete sentence or a sentence fragment. Check (✓) the box in the correct column.

	COMPLETE SENTENCE	SENTENCE FRAGMENT
1. I got a new gadget yesterday.		
2. Research about investments.		
3. Many teenagers like blogging.		
4. Everyone uses social networking sites.		
5. She writing an interesting comment.		
6. My client was extremely interested in the new social networking site.		
7. Cannot share my photos.		
8. Because my favorite podcast about investments.		
9. Last night I listened to a podcast about teen issues.		
10. Very few U.S. teens listening to the radio these days.		

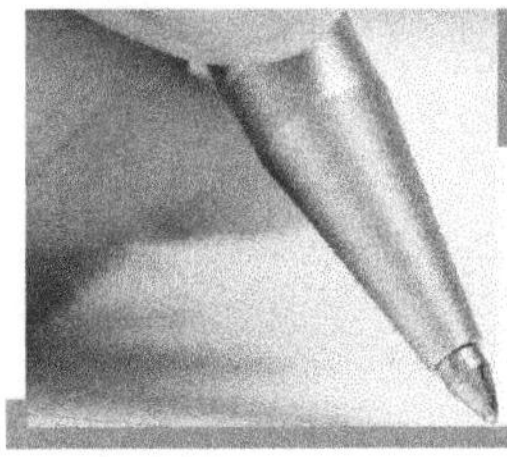

CHECK!

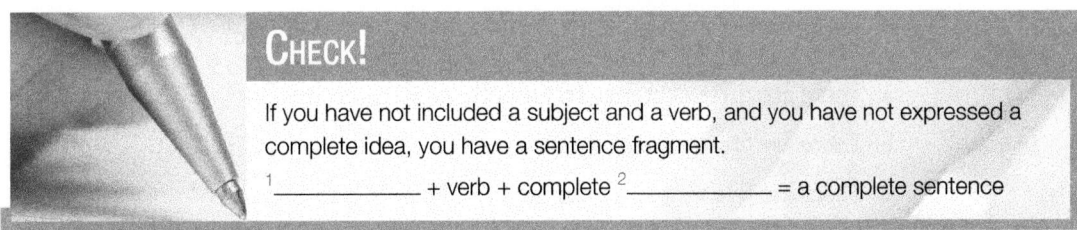

If you have not included a subject and a verb, and you have not expressed a complete idea, you have a sentence fragment.

[1]__________ + verb + complete [2]__________ = a complete sentence

C. Practice

1 Read each sentence and decide if it is a complete sentence or a sentence fragment. Write *CS* for Complete Sentence, *FS* for Fragment without Subject, or *FV* for Fragment without Verb.

___ **1** Downloaded some songs.

___ **2** The blog useful for teenagers.

___ **3** Why doesn't research media jobs?

___ **4** Last weekend, I to the store for a new MP3 player.

___ **5** Podcasts are one way to learn new information about a topic.

___ **6** Blogs a great way to share my ideas.

___ **7** Is hard to predict.

___ **8** Why do you read newspapers?

___ **9** Some people to the radio every day.

___ **10** File sharing common among students.

___ **11** Using podcasts in lectures.

___ **12** It's possible to watch television on computers.

2 Read the paragraph and decide how many sentence fragments there are. Underline them and check the correct answer. Then write *S* for Subject or *V* for Verb, to show what is missing from each one.

Microblogs a good way of keeping in touch with other people. If you have a cell phone with access to the Internet, you can use them. Write microblogs for their friends and family. They also publish news about their activities. Microblogs are a very useful method of communicating for companies, too. Companies can advertise their products with microblogs. Send the information in short messages to customers. In education, some teachers now microblogs in the classroom. Students ask questions, and teachers can quickly give answers or send advice. In general, microblogging an easy way to give a lot of information to a lot of people.

☐ a. There are three sentence fragments. ___ ___ ___

☐ b. There are four sentence fragments. ___ ___ ___ ___

☐ c. There are five sentence fragments. ___ ___ ___ ___ ___

D. Skill Quiz

Check (✓) the correct answer for each item.

1 If a sentence is not complete, it is a sentence ___.

☐ a. false
☐ b. partial
☐ c. fragment

2 A sentence fragment does not have either ___ or a verb.

☐ a. a subject
☐ b. a preposition
☐ c. an adjective

3 *My favorite podcast about music.* This fragment needs a

☐ a. preposition.
☐ b. verb.
☐ c. subject.

4 *Cannot find my photos.* This fragment does not have a

☐ a. subject.
☐ b. preposition.
☐ c. verb.

5 *Microblogs are.* This fragment does not

☐ a. have a subject.
☐ b. express a complete idea.
☐ c. have a verb.

6 Correct this fragment: ___ *are popular among teenagers.*

☐ a. Social networking sites
☐ b. Invest
☐ c. Is

7 Correct this fragment: *You should* ___ *a "friend policy."*

☐ a. ignores
☐ b. prediction
☐ c. have

8 Correct this fragment: ___ *sent me a friend request.*

☐ a. Do
☐ b. My manager
☐ c. To

9 Correct this fragment: ___ *have connections with colleagues.*

☐ a. Many people
☐ b. Are
☐ c. Maintenance

10 Correct this fragment: *Professionals* ___ *learning about social networking sites.*

☐ a. are
☐ b. have
☐ c. blogs

9

CHALLENGING OURSELVES

Topic Sentences

Connecting to the Theme

Do you challenge yourself in school? Read each sentence. Are these statements always, sometimes, or never true for you?

[1]I do many things to stay motivated and organized so I can achieve my academic goals. [2]At the start of every semester, I set goals to improve my grades, one class at a time. [3]Then, each week, I make a study plan in my calendar, and I check off what I achieve each day. [4]I read all the books on my reading list before the semester begins. [5]I meet with my tutor every week to discuss my progress. [6]I study at least two hours each day.

Mostly "always": you really challenge yourself! Remember to give yourself some time off!
Mostly "sometimes": you are motivated and like to challenge yourself, but you are realistic, too.
Mostly "never": you don't challenge yourself much. Try to be more organized.

A. Skill Presentation

A paragraph is a group of sentences about one topic. The **topic sentence** tells the main idea of the paragraph. It is often the first sentence of a paragraph.

Paragraph

- Topic sentence
- Supporting sentences
- Concluding sentence

[T]Many people challenge themselves by making New Year's resolutions. Sometimes they set themselves a goal to lose weight. It is also common to try to eat healthier food. In addition, some people make a resolution to find a better job. Resolutions like these can help people improve their lives.

The topic sentence of this paragraph is *Many people challenge themselves by making New Year's resolutions*. This is the main idea of the paragraph.

The other sentences give details to support the main idea.

B. Over to You

1 Check (✓) the topic sentence and number the sentences in the correct order.

☐ ___ First, I am going to improve my diet.

☐ ___ My New Year's resolution is to lose 20 pounds.

☐ ___ Also, I will go to the gym with a friend.

☐ ___ Next, I will exercise three times a week.

2 Read each paragraph and check (✓) the correct topic sentence.

1 ___ First, I wrote down the main reason that I want to do this. My main reason is to lose weight. Next, I made a menu of what I should eat instead of junk food. My menu includes lean meat, fruits, and vegetables. Finally, I went to the grocery store.

☐ a. My goal this year is to exercise more often.
☐ b. Many people have New Year's resolutions.
☐ c. My New Year's resolution is to eat healthier food.

2 ___ First, write down all of the reasons you think you should make more money. Next, schedule a meeting with your boss. At the meeting, discuss your reasons with your boss. This may help you get a raise.

☐ a. If you want to get a new job, there are some steps you can follow.
☐ b. If your goal is to get a raise at work, you should follow these steps.
☐ c. You should never ask for a raise at work.

3 ___ First, keep a "to do" list and an online calendar. Do the most important things on your daily lists first. Make sure to check your online calendar often. These steps will help you to stay motivated and organized.

☐ a. "To do" lists are not very helpful.
☐ b. Follow these steps if you want to learn how to use the Internet.
☐ c. There are many easy ways to help you get organized.

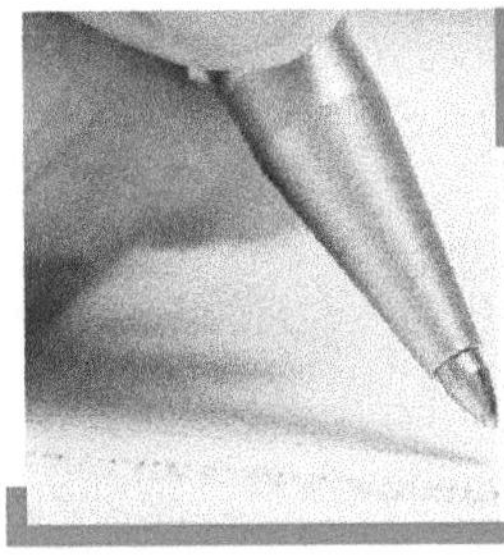

CHECK!

1 All paragraphs have a topic ____________.
2 The topic sentence is often the ____________ sentence of a paragraph.
3 The topic sentence tells us the ____________ idea of the paragraph.
4 The other sentences give details that ____________ the main idea.

C. Practice

1 Number the sentences in the correct order to make logical paragraphs.

1 ___ One main reason is that the resolution is too difficult.
___ Another reason is that people do not stick to their plans.
___ There are many reasons why people do not keep their resolutions.
___ Also, people may not have good support from friends and family.
___ For these reasons, many resolutions are not successful.

2 ___ To reach this goal, you can start by studying more.
___ It is also a good idea to ask questions in class.
___ Getting plenty of sleep may help you do better on tests.
___ If you need additional help, tell your teacher.
___ A common goal is to do better in school.

3 ___ You can be careful about how much trash you throw away.
___ Here are some tips if your goal is to improve the environment.
___ You can also drink tap water instead of buying water in plastic bottles.
___ Finally, you can walk or ride a bike instead of driving more often.
___ These are some easy ways to reach your goal.

2 Read each group of sentences, and check (✓) the best topic sentence.

1 ☐ a. Eat at home instead of at a restaurant.
☐ b. If your New Year's resolution is to save money, follow these steps.
☐ c. Finally, you should not buy things that you do not need.

2 ☐ a. One of my resolutions is to lose 20 pounds.
☐ b. Another resolution I made was to quit smoking.
☐ c. I made many New Year's resolutions this year.

3 ☐ a. Last year, I did not stick to my New Year's resolutions.
☐ b. I felt disappointed with myself.
☐ c. I think my resolutions were too difficult.

4 ☐ a. For example, try to "remember birthdays" instead of "be a better friend."
☐ b. If you want to exercise more, decide exactly how often you will work out.
☐ c. Be specific when making New Year's resolutions.

5 ☐ a. My goal is to exercise at the gym three times a week.
☐ b. First, I am going to choose one exercise class I want to attend.
☐ c. Then I will add the class to my calendar.

6 ☐ a. For example, my co-worker does a daily crossword puzzle.
☐ b. Many people challenge themselves in different ways every day.
☐ c. One of my friends runs several miles each morning.

D. Skill Quiz

Check (✓) the correct answer for each item.

1 What is a paragraph?

☐ a. a complete idea with one subject and one verb
☐ b. a group of sentences about different topics
☐ c. a group of sentences about one topic

2 A topic sentence

☐ a. gives the main idea of the paragraph.
☐ b. explains many details about the topic.
☐ c. comes after the concluding sentence.

3 The topic sentence is often the ___ sentence in a paragraph.

☐ a. first
☐ b. fourth
☐ c. last

4 Choose the topic sentence from a paragraph about a gym's services and equipment.

☐ a. You can attend classes between 7 a.m. and 10 p.m.
☐ b. You can use free weights, treadmills, and exercise machines.
☐ c. We offer many ways for you to achieve your fitness goals.

5 Choose the topic sentence from a paragraph about resolutions.

☐ a. For example, some people want to lose weight.
☐ b. Some people want to get a better job.
☐ c. Many people make New Year's resolutions.

6 Choose the topic sentence from a paragraph about problems.

☐ a. For example, if you are angry with a friend, talk to them about it.
☐ b. As a result, you could create stress in your life.
☐ c. You should face your problems, not ignore them.

7 Choose the topic sentence from a paragraph about smoking.

☐ a. In addition, many people do not like the way it smells.
☐ b. In my opinion, smoking should not be allowed in public.
☐ c. It is not fair to people who do not want to breathe smoke.

8 Choose the topic sentence from a paragraph about interviews.

☐ a. There are many qualities that can help you be successful at a job interview.
☐ b. For example, you should be confident.
☐ c. A person also needs to be friendly at the interview.

9 Choose the topic sentence from a paragraph about studying.

☐ a. There are several steps to follow in order to study for a test.
☐ b. First, you should make a study plan.
☐ c. Then you should choose a quiet place to study.

10 Choose the topic sentence from a paragraph about volunteering.

☐ a. One reason is that you can make new friends.
☐ b. There are many reasons you should volunteer.
☐ c. Also, you can gain job experience as a volunteer.

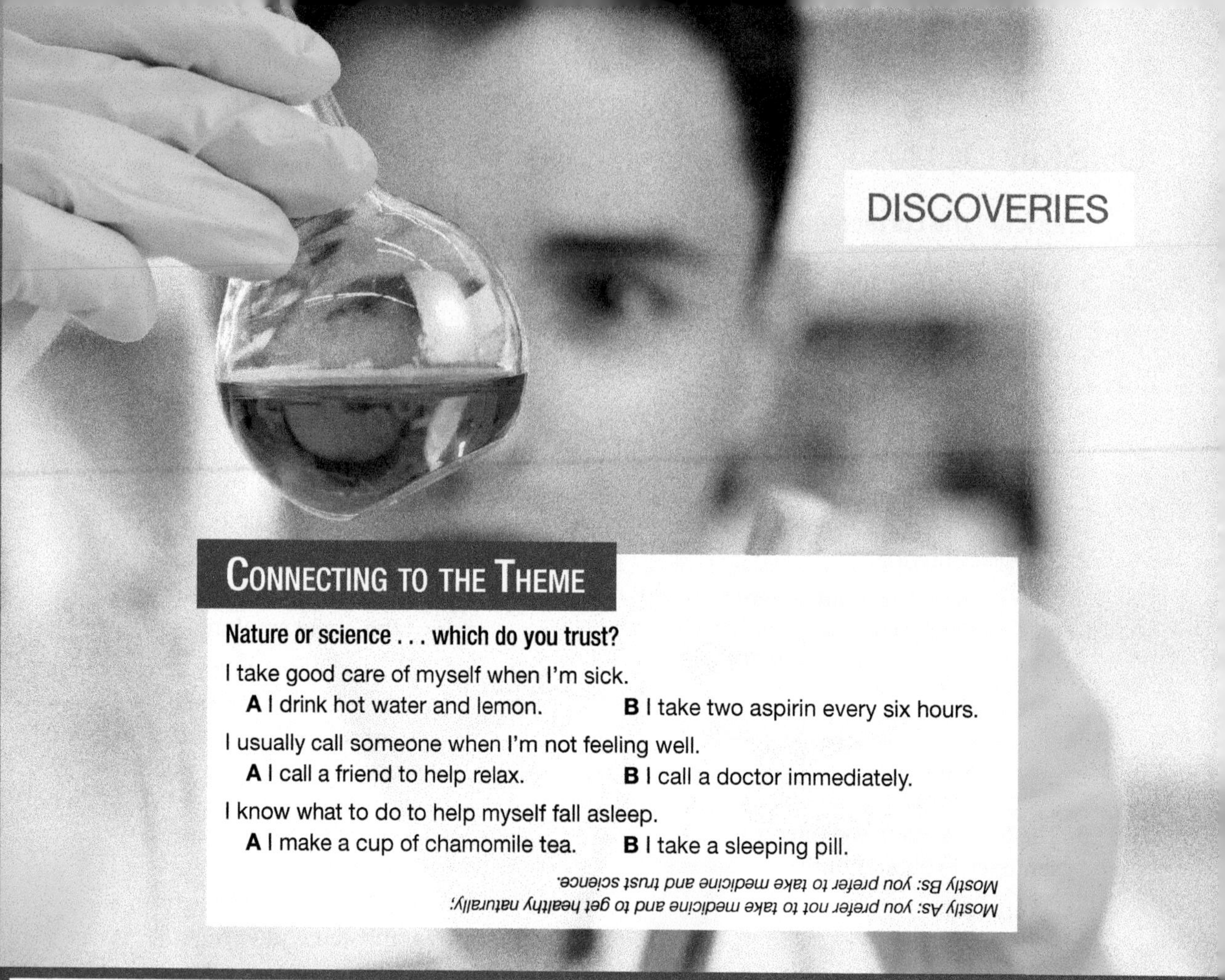

DISCOVERIES

Connecting to the Theme

Nature or science . . . which do you trust?

I take good care of myself when I'm sick.
A I drink hot water and lemon. **B** I take two aspirin every six hours.

I usually call someone when I'm not feeling well.
A I call a friend to help relax. **B** I call a doctor immediately.

I know what to do to help myself fall asleep.
A I make a cup of chamomile tea. **B** I take a sleeping pill.

Mostly As: you prefer not to take medicine and to get healthy naturally;
Mostly Bs: you prefer to take medicine and trust science.

A. Skill Presentation

The topic sentence in a paragraph gives the main idea. The body of a paragraph is made up of sentences that give more information about the main idea. These are called **supporting sentences**.

Paragraph
- **Topic sentence**
- **Supporting sentences**
- Concluding sentence

Good supporting sentences are:
- related to the topic sentence
- specific
- often include examples

Read the topic sentence and the sentences that follow.

[T]Olive oil has a number of health benefits. [S]It has important vitamins that are good for your body. ~~Olives are common in countries near the Mediterranean Sea.~~ [S]People who use olive oil regularly may be less likely to get some diseases. [S]Chemicals in olive oil may actually prevent cancer. [S]The fat in olive oil is healthy and can lower the risk for heart disease. ~~Olive oil is full of flavor and smells nice, too.~~

The crossed out sentences are not supporting sentences because they are not specific examples related to the topic sentence. They provide more information about olives but not about the health benefits of olives.

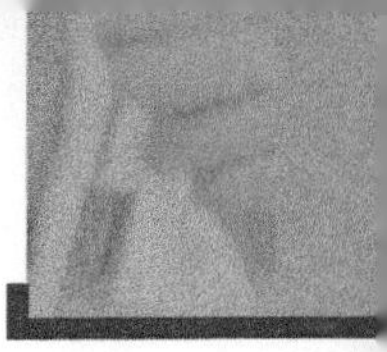

B. Over to You

1 Read the topic sentence and underline the two supporting sentences.

Biologists are researching how the acai berry can improve health. [1]Scientists think the acai berry could improve heart health. [2]Many people think the acai berry tastes good. [3]Some people eat them for breakfast with other berries. [4]The acai berry might also help people live longer. [5]The berries grow on palm trees.

2 Read the two topic sentences and the supporting sentences in the chart. Decide which topic sentence each one supports. Check (✓) the box in the correct column.

Topic Sentence A: Some health discoveries may help people live longer.

Topic Sentence B: Some health discoveries help people deal with pain.

	TOPIC SENTENCE A	TOPIC SENTENCE B
1. Certain drugs might add years to a person's life.		
2. Aspirin is a common medicine for headaches.		
3. Research shows that people who eat less may die at an older age.		
4. If your back hurts, stretching and relaxation can help.		
5. Some organisms in the ocean make chemicals that can help with muscle aches.		
6. Acai berries may be good for the heart.		
7. Scientists in Denmark discovered that exercise contributes to good health for older people.		
8. Doctors in England found that chili peppers can sometimes help arthritis pain.		
9. One study found that people who sleep six to seven hours a night may live to be older.		
10. Indian researchers studied the effects of yoga on back pain.		

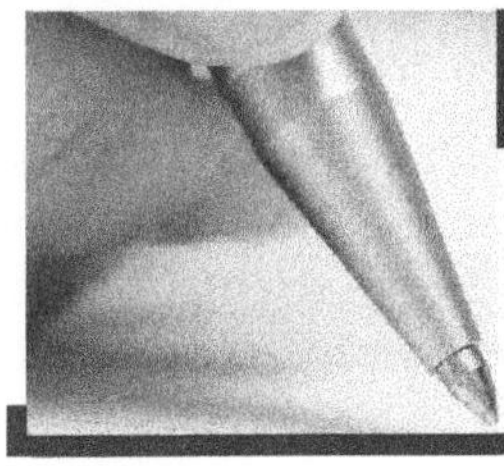

CHECK!

1 Supporting sentences are related to the ____________ sentence.

2 Supporting sentences are usually ____________ and often include ____________.

C. Practice

1 Read each topic sentence and check (✓) the correct supporting sentence.

1 Biologists have discovered medicine in many places in the world.

☐ a. When people get a disease, they have to go to the hospital for treatment.
☐ b. Some of these drugs come from chemicals in the ocean.
☐ c. It is important to take medicine that your doctor gives you.

2 Different kinds of medicine have been found in coral reefs in the ocean.

☐ a. Chemicals used to treat cancer were discovered in coral reefs.
☐ b. Divers enjoy exploring coral reefs because they are often very beautiful.
☐ c. Biologists continue to look for medicine in the Amazon rainforest.

3 Some people think green tea slows the aging process.

☐ a. You can stay healthy by exercising and eating right.
☐ b. Drinking it frequently may help you live longer.
☐ c. My 90-year-old grandmother adds honey to her tea.

4 The discovery of penicillin is important for many reasons.

☐ a. Aspirin helps many people deal with pain.
☐ b. Doctors use many different drugs to treat diseases.
☐ c. Penicillin saves lives every year by treating different diseases.

5 Scientists visit many places to discover new medical treatments.

☐ a. Dr. Wu looks for medicine in the ocean.
☐ b. Dr. O'Dell vacations in South America every year.
☐ c. When I feel sick, I go to the doctor to get medicine.

6 The acai berry may be good for your health.

☐ a. It can make your immune system stronger so you do not get sick.
☐ b. Acai berries are delicious.
☐ c. My sister feels sick because she ate too much blueberry pie.

7 Many people do not like to take medicine.

☐ a. They know that smoking can make you sick.
☐ b. Instead, they look at websites about drugs when they get sick.
☐ c. Instead, they might eat chicken soup or drink hot tea when they get sick.

2 Read the topic sentence. How many supporting sentences are there?

Researchers have found that vitamin D has many health benefits. [1]First of all, this vitamin helps your body fight off diseases. [2]Vitamin C may prevent the common cold. [3]One study found that vitamin D can also lower people's blood pressure. [4]Some scientists have even found that vitamin D could prevent cancer. [5]Exercising every day can lead to health benefits. [6]Most doctors agree that healthy bones need vitamin D.

There are ___ supporting sentences in the paragraph. Sentences: ___________

D. Skill Quiz

Check (✓) the correct answer for each item.

1 Which statement describes a good supporting sentence?

- ☐ a. It always comes at the beginning of a paragraph.
- ☐ b. It gives more information about the topic sentence.
- ☐ c. It is the only sentence in a paragraph.

2 Supporting sentences often include

- ☐ a. conclusions.
- ☐ b. main ideas.
- ☐ c. examples.

3 *A fruit found in Asia, mangosteen, has many health benefits.*
Which supporting sentence goes with this topic sentence?

- ☐ a. Fruits found in South America have important health benefits.
- ☐ b. Some doctors believe that chemicals in it could prevent cancer.
- ☐ c. Mangosteen juice is very expensive.

4 *Medical researchers visit different locations to find new kinds of medicine.*
Which supporting sentence goes with this topic sentence?

- ☐ a. Some medical teams found cancer-fighting drugs in the Arctic Ocean.
- ☐ b. The Arctic is also home to animals such as polar bears.
- ☐ c. New drugs have to be tested many times to make sure they are safe.

5 *Biologists found that garlic is a useful natural medicine.*
Which supporting sentence goes with this topic sentence?

- ☐ a. Garlic is a very popular food around the world.
- ☐ b. Chemicals in yogurt can help people stay well.
- ☐ c. Chemicals in garlic can prevent heart disease.

6 *People eat goji berries for a variety of health reasons.*
Which supporting sentence goes with this topic sentence?

- ☐ a. Goji berries can be found in China.
- ☐ b. Goji berries may help you see better.
- ☐ c. Goji berries are bright red and are usually dried.

7 *Technology can help people stay healthy.*
Which supporting sentence goes with this topic sentence?

- ☐ a. Some cell phones help you count calories.
- ☐ b. Blueberries have been shown to help people lose weight.
- ☐ c. Yogurt has powerful chemicals to aid in food digestion.

8 *There are more than 8,000 kinds of plants in African forests.*
Which supporting sentence goes with this topic sentence?

- ☐ a. Scientists do not know the exact number of organisms that live in the ocean.
- ☐ b. Walnut trees and African tulips are two plants found in these forests.
- ☐ c. Animals such as zebras live in other parts of Africa.

11

Concluding Sentences

UNSOLVED MYSTERIES

Connecting to the Theme

Are you benefitting from the real power of your dreams? Read this paragraph. Are the numbered statements true or false for you?

Scientists are discovering that dreams may help us with our studies. For instance, [1]some students take a short nap during the day. Research now shows that this can help them remember what they learned before the nap! This is especially true if they dream about it, as dreams are a sign that the brain is processing the new information. [2]Also, a lot of students tend to study late at night, just before sleeping. Scientists now believe this improves memory. [3]They also found that some students even remember dreaming about their work when they wake the next day. This research has not solved the complete mystery of why we dream, but scientists are finding out how dreaming can help us learn.

Mostly true: you are making the most of your dreams. Mostly false: you should listen to the latest scientific research and let your dreams improve your studies.

A. Skill Presentation

The **concluding sentence** is usually the last sentence in a paragraph. A concluding sentence can repeat the main idea of the paragraph (from the topic sentence) using different words. It may start with "In conclusion".

Paragraph

- **Topic sentence**
- **Supporting sentences**
- **Concluding sentence**

Read this paragraph about scientists studying why some people feel better when taking fake medicine (known as the placebo effect).

> [T]Scientists are working hard to understand the placebo effect. [S]The placebo effect is when patients get better without drugs or other medical treatment. [S]Patients believe they are taking medicine to get better, and they do get better. [S]In reality, they are taking a sugar pill – a placebo. [S]Scientists are not sure how this works. [S]They are studying the brain to find out. [S]If they can explain the placebo effect, they believe they could help some sick people get better just by using their brains. [C]It is not difficult to see why scientists are trying to solve this mystery.

The concluding sentence repeats the idea of the topic sentence but uses different words.

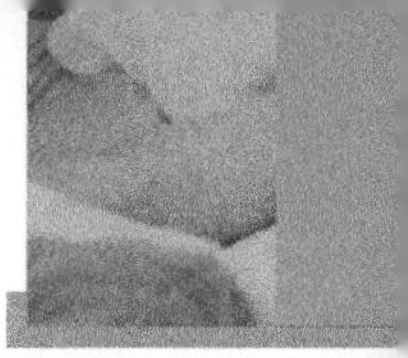

B. Over to You

1 Read the topic sentence from a paragraph about yawning, and check (✓) the correct concluding sentence.

Topic Sentence: Why people yawn is an unsolved scientific mystery.

Concluding Sentence:

☐ a. People yawn when they are tired.
☐ b. Scientists still are not sure why people yawn.
☐ c. Another unsolved scientific mystery is why people sleepwalk.

2 Match each topic sentence (1–5) with two correct concluding sentences (a–j).

1 There are many unsolved mysteries of the brain. ___ ___

2 One theory says your brain examines the day's problems during sleep. ___ ___

3 The brain has areas for short-term memory and long-term memory. ___ ___

4 Many elderly people cannot remember things that happened recently. ___ ___

5 There are many theories about why people walk in their sleep. ___ ___

a In conclusion, scientists do not completely understand how the brain works.

b In conclusion, this theory states that sleep is a time for the brain to think about problems.

c The theory states that the brain may be able to solve problems as you sleep.

d Scientists give different reasons to explain why people might sleepwalk.

e There are still things scientists do not know about how the brain works.

f In conclusion, as people get older, it is more difficult to remember recent events.

g In conclusion, the brain keeps short-and long-term memories in different places.

h In conclusion, sleepwalking could be caused by a number of different things.

i Older people might have trouble remembering something that just happened.

j Different memories are kept in different areas of the brain.

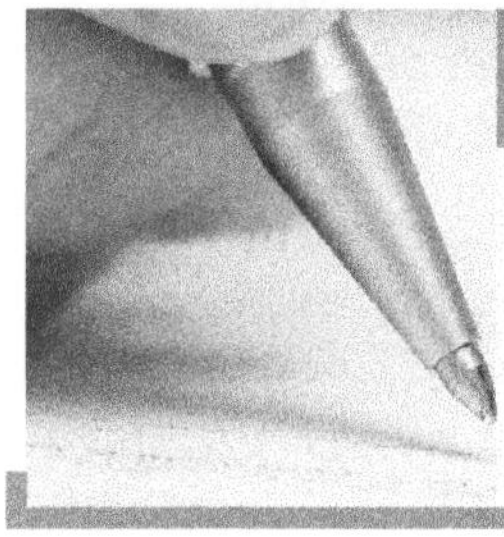

CHECK!

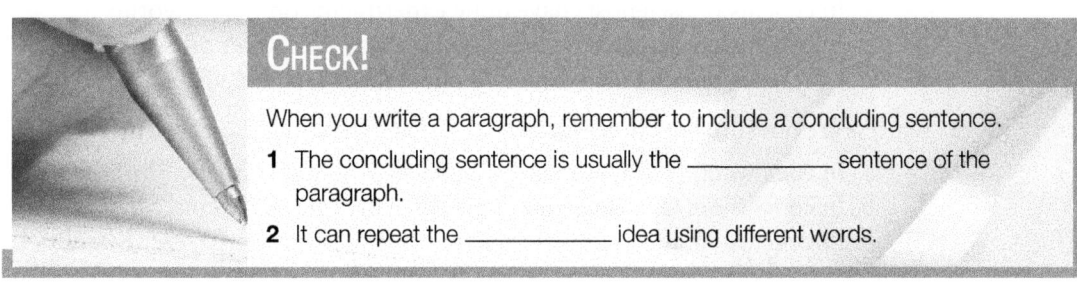

When you write a paragraph, remember to include a concluding sentence.

1 The concluding sentence is usually the ____________ sentence of the paragraph.

2 It can repeat the ____________ idea using different words.

C. Practice

1 Read each paragraph and check (✓) the correct concluding sentence.

1 Many scientists are confused about the disappearance of a lake in Chile. In 2007, a huge lake in Chile was suddenly gone. In its place was a hole with a large piece of ice in it. Some scientists think that an earthquake made the lake disappear. Other scientists think that global warming is the cause. ___

- [ ] a. In conclusion, some people think the ice melted.
- [ ] b. In conclusion, scientists are not sure what happened to the lake.

2 For years, people have wondered why the Tower of Pisa leans, and now there is an answer. As soon as the tower was finished in the 1300s, it started to tilt, or lean. By 1989, it was leaning 4.5 meters from its center. For years, some people wondered if the tower leaned because of the way it was built. Finally, the mystery was solved. The tower started leaning because the ground under it is very soft. ___

- [ ] a. There is finally an answer to the mystery of why Pisa's tower leans.
- [ ] b. John Burland spent 20 years trying to understand the mystery of the tower.

2 Read each topic sentence and check (✓) the correct concluding sentence.

1 Some scientists think birds use magnetic fields to prevent them from getting lost.

- [ ] a. In conclusion, scientists have proved why birds do not get lost.
- [ ] b. In conclusion, birds might not get lost because they can use magnetic fields.
- [ ] c. In conclusion, some birds travel thousands of miles every year.

2 Photographs show blue and white lights flashing in the sky before an earthquake.

- [ ] a. Researchers have not found the cause of the blue and white lights.
- [ ] b. The photos show that colored lights occur before earthquakes.
- [ ] c. Green lights also appear in the sky in many northern countries.

3 Some dogs can sense when people have diseases.

- [ ] a. One dog knew that its owner had a serious disease.
- [ ] b. Dogs can also comfort sick people.
- [ ] c. Some dogs can detect illnesses in sick people.

4 The recent discovery of a meteorite might prove there was once life on Mars.

- [ ] a. In conclusion, scientists have done experiments on the meteorite.
- [ ] b. In conclusion, scientists wonder if there was ever water on Mars.
- [ ] c. In conclusion, this meteorite may show that Mars had life in the past.

5 Experts are not sure how the Nazca Lines in Peru were made.

- [ ] a. In conclusion, the lines make pictures of different animals.
- [ ] b. In conclusion, experts do not know how the lines were created.
- [ ] c. In conclusion, the lines were probably made more than 2,000 years ago.

6 Bee stings may be able to cure one common disease.

- [ ] a. Bee stings might help cure a disease that many people have.
- [ ] b. This type of treatment is called venom therapy.
- [ ] c. People with allergies should avoid bee stings.

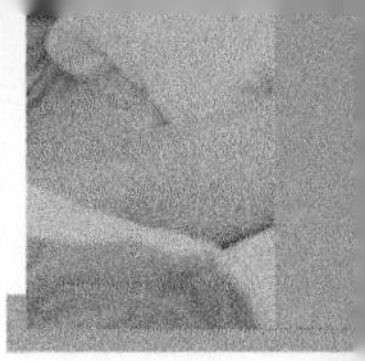

D. Skill Quiz

Check (✓) the correct answer for each item.

1 Where is a concluding sentence usually found?

- ☐ a. at the beginning of a paragraph
- ☐ b. in the middle of a paragraph
- ☐ c. at the end of a paragraph

2 What is one way to write a concluding sentence?

- ☐ a. Repeat the main idea.
- ☐ b. Repeat most of the supporting sentences.
- ☐ c. Give new information.

3 What can you do when you write a concluding sentence?

- ☐ a. Copy the topic sentence exactly.
- ☐ b. Restate the topic sentence with different words.
- ☐ c. Write a new idea about the topic.

4 Which phrase can start a concluding sentence?

- ☐ a. First of all,
- ☐ b. Next,
- ☐ c. In conclusion,

5 Choose the concluding sentence for this topic sentence: *People dream during Rapid Eye Movement (REM) sleep.*

- ☐ a. In conclusion, REM stands for Rapid Eye Movement.
- ☐ b. In conclusion, dreams happen during REM sleep.
- ☐ c. In conclusion, many people do not remember their dreams.

6 Choose the concluding sentence for this topic sentence: *Average people sometimes show great strength in a crisis.*

- ☐ a. For example, a mother once lifted a car to save her baby.
- ☐ b. Scientists are not sure why.
- ☐ c. A person's physical power often increases in times of stress.

7 Choose the concluding sentence for this topic sentence: *Most people need at least eight hours of sleep every night to be healthy.*

- ☐ a. In conclusion, it can be dangerous to not sleep for several days.
- ☐ b. In conclusion, doctors recommend that their patients sleep for about eight hours a night.
- ☐ c. In conclusion, scientists know why some people cannot sleep at night.

8 Choose the concluding sentence for this topic sentence: *Some researchers think the Nazca Lines prove people had ways to fly.*

- ☐ a. It may be possible to make lines like them using an airplane.
- ☐ b. Scientists from all over the world study the Nazca Lines.
- ☐ c. People may have had ways to fly, and some researchers think the Nazca Lines show this.

9 Choose the concluding sentence for this topic sentence: *There are cures for many diseases, but some diseases do not have cures.*

- ☐ a. In conclusion, certain diseases can be cured, but others cannot.
- ☐ b. In conclusion, scientists want to find cures for all diseases.
- ☐ c. In conclusion, aspirin can help stop headaches.

10 Choose the concluding sentence for this topic sentence: *Many illnesses can be cured without medicine.*

- ☐ a. There are ways to get better without drugs.
- ☐ b. Some illnesses may never have a cure.
- ☐ c. Some doctors should find new jobs.

12

Sentences with Relative Clauses

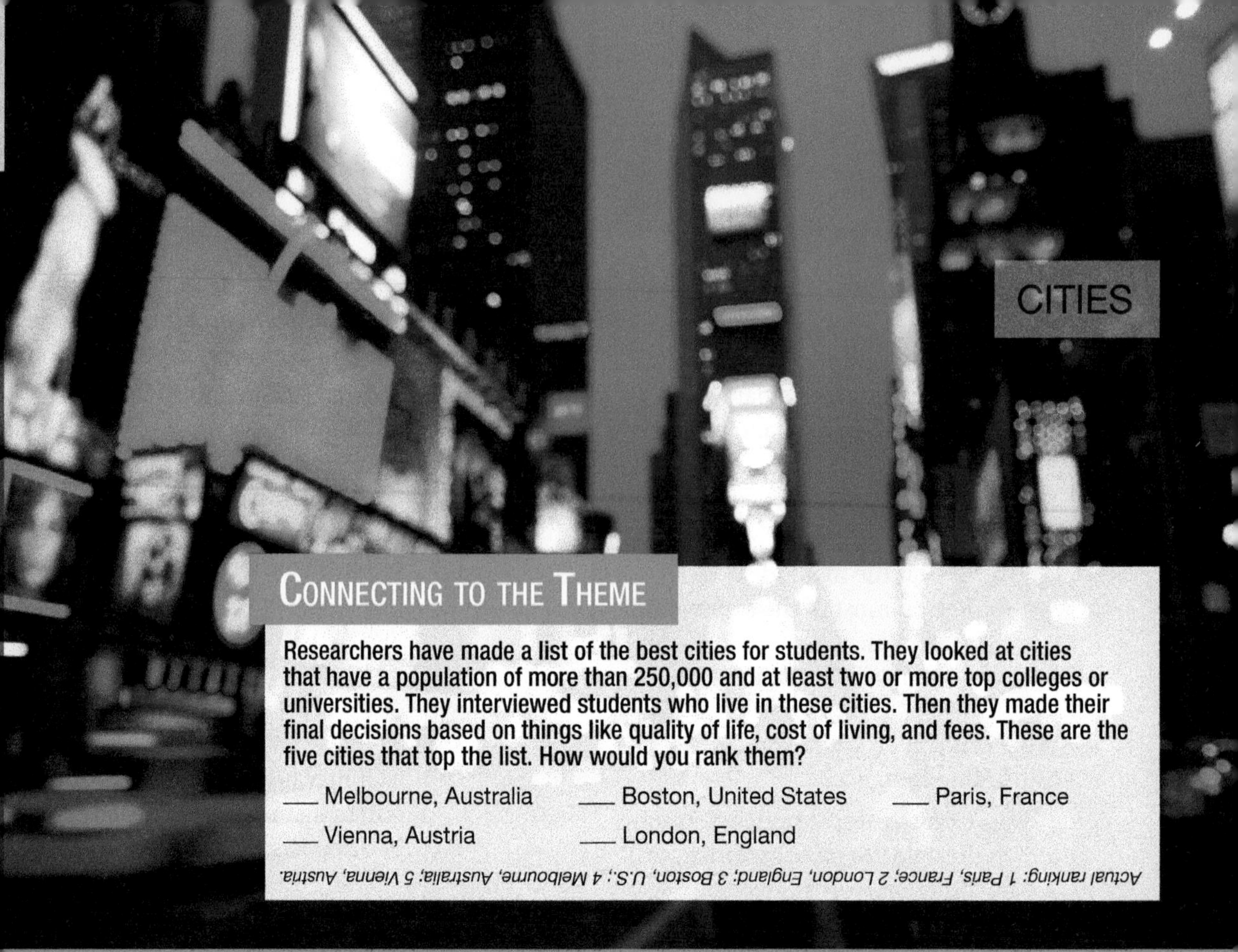

CITIES

Connecting to the Theme

Researchers have made a list of the best cities for students. They looked at cities that have a population of more than 250,000 and at least two or more top colleges or universities. They interviewed students who live in these cities. Then they made their final decisions based on things like quality of life, cost of living, and fees. These are the five cities that top the list. How would you rank them?

___ Melbourne, Australia ___ Boston, United States ___ Paris, France

___ Vienna, Austria ___ London, England

Actual ranking: 1 Paris, France; 2 London, England; 3 Boston, U.S.; 4 Melbourne, Australia; 5 Vienna, Austria.

A. Skill Presentation

An independent clause is a complete sentence. It has a subject and a verb, and it expresses a complete idea.

Tokyo is a city in Japan.

A dependent clause is not a complete sentence. It does not express a complete idea. A **relative clause**, also called an adjective clause, is one kind of dependent clause. It describes a noun or gives more information about it.

that has more than 28 million people (We do not know what has more than 28 million people.)

When we write, we can connect a **relative clause** to an **independent clause** to give more information and make a complete sentence.

— INDEPENDENT CLAUSE — ——— RELATIVE CLAUSE ———

Tokyo is a city in Japan that has more than 28 million people.

The relative clause *that has more than 28 million people* describes the noun *city*. It gives us more information about what kind of city Tokyo is.

Relative clauses can begin with *that*, *which*, or *who*. Relative clauses that describe things can begin with *that* or *which*.

Tokyo is a city that / which has more than 28 million people.

An *urban planner* is a kind of person. Relative clauses that describe people can begin with *who* or *that*.

Urban planners are people who / that design cities.

B. Over to You

1 Match each relative clause (1–5) with the correct independent clause (a–e).

1 Dr. Vu is the professor ___

2 This is the map ___

3 There are people ___

4 It is a city ___

5 Ms. Lin is the principal ___

a that work in green buildings.

b which has a large population.

c who is responsible for the largest school district.

d that shows the tourist destinations.

e who teaches urban planning.

2 Read the paragraph. How many relative clauses are there?

> [1]Mumbai is a city which has a population of almost 14 million people. [2]It the largest city in India, and it is one of the world's megacities. [3]There are problems in Mumbai, including slums and poverty. [4]There are also places in Mumbai that have wonderful things to do. [5]For example, Mumbai has many interesting museums. [6]Many kinds of people live in Mumbai because people from all over India have migrated to the city. [7]Mumbai's population is increasing rapidly, so transportation in the city is a problem. [8]The Mumbai Urban Transportation Project is a system that may help Mumbai's transportation problems. [9]It will provide more railroads, buses, and subways. [10]There are also plans to build more roads and bridges. [11]Many people who are experts in urban planning are involved in the project.

There are ___ relative clauses. Sentences: ____________

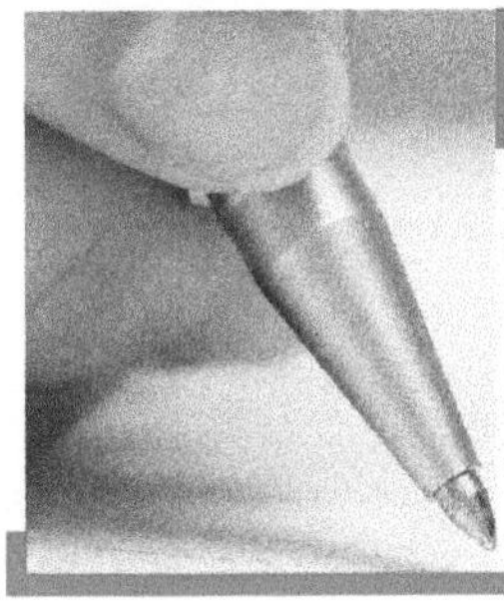

CHECK!

1 A ____________ clause is one kind of dependent clause. It describes a noun.

2 It can start with *that*, ____________, or *who*.

3 It must be connected to an ____________ clause to make a complete sentence.

C. Practice

1 Read each item in the chart. Decide if it is an independent clause or a dependent (relative) clause. Check (✓) the box in the correct column.

	INDEPENDENT CLAUSE	RELATIVE CLAUSE
1. An architect designs buildings.		
2. That are good for the environment.		
3. Ms. Sheldon is an urban planner.		
4. Which are megacities.		
5. Which is in the United States.		
6. Tokyo is the largest megacity.		
7. Who is an urban planner.		
8. Slums are often in megacities.		
9. Mumbai is in India.		
10. That designed many green buildings.		

2 Match each independent clause (1–8) with the correct relative clause (a–h) to make complete sentences.

1 There are many cities in the world ___

2 Corvallis is a green city ___

3 Will Wynn was a mayor in Texas ___

4 Corvallis is home to many people ___

5 Austin and Dallas are cities ___

6 The Emerald Express in Oregon is a bus system ___

7 She is an architect ___

8 My family and I are people ___

a who designs buildings in Portland.

b which are in Texas.

c that won a transportation award.

d that is in Oregon.

e who helped make his city green.

f that are raising our children to respect the environment.

g which are green cities.

h who work together to keep the city clean.

D. Skill Quiz

Check (✓) the correct answer for each item.

1 What is an independent clause?

☐ a. a complete sentence
☐ b. an incomplete idea
☐ c. a fragment that describes a noun

2 A dependent clause

☐ a. is the same thing as a complete sentence.
☐ b. does not express a complete idea.
☐ c. is never a fragment.

3 To make a complete sentence, a dependent clause must be connected to

☐ a. an independent clause.
☐ b. a relative clause.
☐ c. another dependent clause.

4 What does a relative clause describe?

☐ a. a verb
☐ b. a fragment
☐ c. a noun

5 Which words can start relative clauses that describe things?

☐ a. *that* or *which*
☐ b. *that* or *who*
☐ c. *who* or *which*

6 Which words can start relative clauses that describe people?

☐ a. *that* or *which*
☐ b. *that* or *who*
☐ c. *who* or *which*

7 Choose the relative clause.

☐ a. Wangari Maathai is the Kenyan woman who started the Green Belt Movement.
☐ b. GBM is an abbreviation for the Green Belt Movement.
☐ c. Who started the Green Belt Movement in 1977.

8 Choose the independent clause.

☐ a. GBM is an organization in Kenya.
☐ b. That protects the environment.
☐ c. Which began over 30 years ago.

9 *People that work for GBM help people around the world.*
In this sentence, which word can replace *that*?

☐ a. which
☐ b. who
☐ c. what

10 *GBM planted trees that will help Kenya's forests grow.*
In this sentence, which word can replace *that*?

☐ a. which
☐ b. who
☐ c. what

13

Simple vs. Compound Sentences

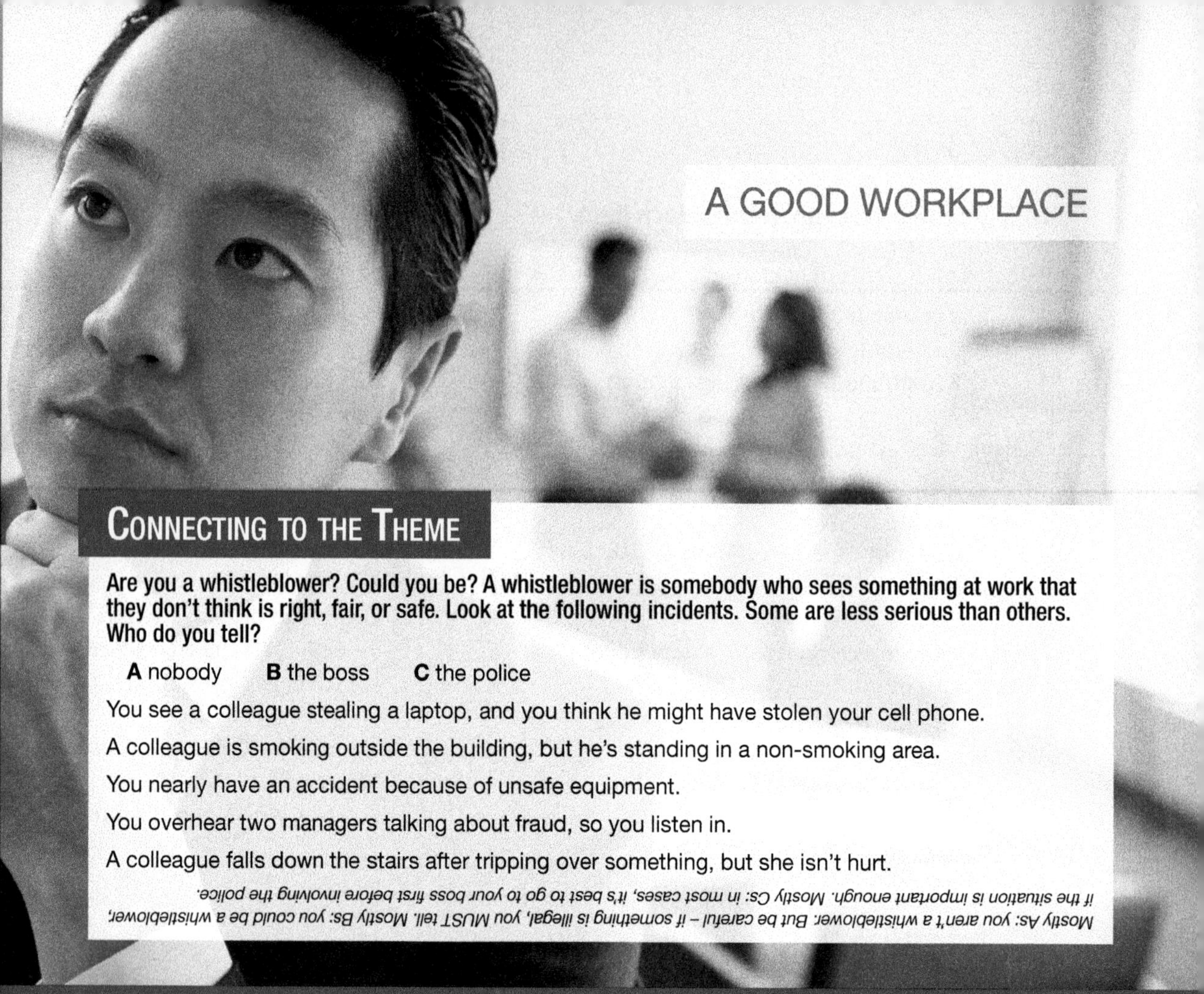

A GOOD WORKPLACE

Connecting to the Theme

Are you a whistleblower? Could you be? A whistleblower is somebody who sees something at work that they don't think is right, fair, or safe. Look at the following incidents. Some are less serious than others. Who do you tell?

A nobody **B** the boss **C** the police

You see a colleague stealing a laptop, and you think he might have stolen your cell phone.

A colleague is smoking outside the building, but he's standing in a non-smoking area.

You nearly have an accident because of unsafe equipment.

You overhear two managers talking about fraud, so you listen in.

A colleague falls down the stairs after tripping over something, but she isn't hurt.

Mostly As: you aren't a whistleblower. But be careful – if something is illegal, you MUST tell. Mostly Bs: you could be a whistleblower, if the situation is important enough. Mostly Cs: in most cases, it's best to go to your boss first before involving the police.

A. Skill Presentation

An independent clause has a subject and a verb, and it expresses a complete idea. A **simple sentence** has one independent clause.

Whistleblowers report illegal or unethical behavior.

They can talk about broken safety rules.

Two simple sentences can be combined to make a **compound sentence** using a conjunction. Compound sentences can help make your writing more interesting.

Whistleblowers report illegal or unethical behavior, **and** they can talk about broken safety rules.

Follow these three steps to make a compound sentence:

1 Make sure the simple sentences are related. Only sentences that are closely related can be combined.

2 Add a conjunction between the independent clauses. Conjunctions have different meanings. Remember to use the conjunction with the correct meaning.

and (similar idea)	but (opposite idea)
or (another possibility)	so (a result that is not surprising)

3 Change the period at the end of the first independent clause to a comma.

B. Over to You

1 Some of these compound sentences have mistakes. Write *C* for Correct or *I* for Incorrect.

___ 1 Whistleblowers may help fix problems, or my boss treats employees fairly.

___ 2 Whistleblowers talk to people inside the company, or they talk to people outside the company.

___ 3 Whistleblowers see a problem they report it.

2 Match each independent clause (1–8) with the correct dependent clause (a–h) to make compound sentences.

1 Whistleblowers are trying to be helpful, ___

2 You have the right to report discrimination, ___

3 Whistleblowers talk to someone working for the company, ___

4 Most people do not like to feel humiliated, ___

5 Good training can help employees know their rights, ___

6 An unsafe condition may be using a dangerous machine, ___

7 Problems at work should be reported, ___

8 Reporting problems should be easy, ___

a and it can help them learn new skills.

b and you are allowed to report other major problems.

c or it may be working with sharp objects.

d but they often face discrimination.

e so they avoid embarrassing situations.

f and they should be fixed quickly.

g but it is sometimes difficult.

h or they talk to someone else.

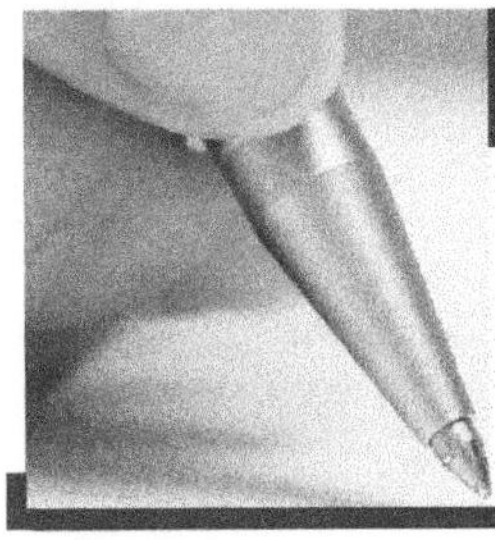

CHECK!

1 Make sure the sentences are ___________.

2 Add a ___________ such as *and*, *but*, *or*, or *so*.

3 Change the period at the end of the first independent clause to a ___________.

C. Practice

1 Circle the correct conjunction for each compound sentence.

1 Employees need to know how to use dangerous machinery, *so* | *and* | *but* they should ask for training.

2 Paulo does the same job as Magda, *so* | *and* | *but* he makes more money.

3 The new worker did not like working with chemicals, *so* | *and* | *but* he did not like loud noise.

4 It is legal to report bad conditions to your boss, *so* | *and* | *but* you can report them to an agency.

5 My boss trained me how to use the machines, *so* | *and* | *but* he taught me safety rules.

6 I did not listen to my boss explain the rules, *so* | *and* | *but* I do not know what to do.

7 Mistakes are not good, *so* | *and* | *but* they can be fixed sometimes.

2 Read each item in the chart and decide if the sentence is correct or if it has an error. Check (✓) the box in the correct column.

	CORRECT	WRONG CONJUNCTION	UNRELATED INDEPENDENT CLAUSES
1. I work with dangerous materials, or I get special training.			
2. The employees are from many countries, but there is no discrimination.			
3. My coworker feels humiliated, and my company offers computer training.			
4. I like the company, but I am not going to leave.			
5. Workers use dangerous machines, so they take training classes.			
6. I like my boss, and certain chemicals can be dangerous.			
7. Marie makes the same amount of money as Deniz, but they receive different treatment.			
8. Juan understands workers' rights, and smoking is unhealthy.			
9. My boss taught me about the machine, or she gave me a book about it.			

D. Skill Quiz

Check (✓) the correct answer for each item.

1 A simple sentence has ___ independent clause(s).

☐ a. one
☐ b. two
☐ c. three

2 A compound sentence always has more than one

☐ a. conjunction.
☐ b. comma.
☐ c. independent clause.

3 Complete this sentence: *Nina will get training, ___ she will learn new skills.*

☐ a. but
☐ b. so
☐ c. or

4 Complete this sentence: *Companies should be ethical, ___ they should have good working conditions.*

☐ a. and
☐ b. or
☐ c. but

5 Complete this sentence: *There is no discrimination at my company, ___ the working conditions are not very good.*

☐ a. but
☐ b. or
☐ c. so

6 *My company treats people fairly and pays men and women the same amount.*
This sentence needs a

☐ a. pronoun.
☐ b. conjunction.
☐ c. comma.

7 *Some people think whistleblowers are good, and I work with people from many countries.*
This sentence needs

☐ a. a conjunction.
☐ b. related clauses.
☐ c. a comma.

8 *Nestor's company is a nice place to work, it has good conditions.*
This sentence needs a

☐ a. clause.
☐ b. preposition.
☐ c. conjunction.

9 *She wanted the same treatment so she was happy that she was treated like her co-workers.*
This sentence needs

☐ a. a different conjunction.
☐ b. another clause.
☐ c. a comma.

10 *It's important to report unethical behavior, but the unethical behavior will continue.*
This sentence needs

☐ a. another comma.
☐ b. a different conjunction.
☐ c. a preposition.

14 Complex Sentences

LEARN QUICKLY!

Connecting to the Theme

People learn in different ways. Read these pairs of sentences. Which pair expresses you most?

A When a tutor is giving a presentation, I prefer to look at the screen.
I'd rather watch a video than listen to a podcast.

B I prefer to move around the classroom during lessons rather than sit still.
I like to carry out practical experiments after reading about a subject.

C I'd rather not read the text book if I can listen to a lecture instead.
I always like to ask questions and join in discussions in class.

A: seeing things is important to you when you study – you may be a visual learner; B: you like to be active when you learn – you may be a kinesthetic learner; C: you learn best by listening – you may be an auditory learner.

A. Skill Presentation

A sentence created by combining an independent clause (a complete sentence) and a dependent clause (not a complete sentence) is called a **complex sentence**. Good writing includes a mix of simple, compound, and complex sentences. If you include complex sentences in your writing, people will find your writing more interesting and more enjoyable to read.

In a complex sentence, a dependent clause often begins with a subordinating conjunction. For example, in this sentence, *because* is the subordinating conjunction.

INDEPENDENT CLAUSE — **DEPENDENT CLAUSE**

Visual learners often like charts because they learn best by looking at things.

Four common subordinating conjunctions are *after*, *because*, *if*, and *when*.

The independent clause does not always come first. The dependent clause can also come first. For example, look at these two sentences:

IC — **DC**

He learns new words more easily when he hears them in sentences.

DC — **IC**

When he hears new words in sentences, he learns them more easily.

Notice that when the dependent clause comes first, it is followed by a comma.

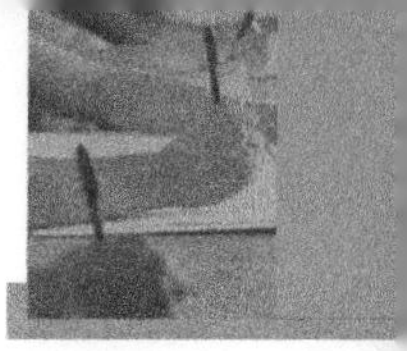

B. Over to You

1 Circle the subordinating conjunctions.

1 You will understand better after you read the book.

2 The students will do well on the test if they study hard.

3 He learns more easily when he hears them in sentences.

4 I am very tired today because I stayed up late studying last night.

2 Read each sentence in the chart and decide if it is simple or complex. Check (✓) the box in the correct column.

	SIMPLE SENTENCE	COMPLEX SENTENCE
1. I am a kinesthetic learner.		
2. When he does actual activities, he learns the material better.		
3. You will not pass the test if you do not study.		
4. My father is going to meet me at 7:00.		
5. He is not going to meet me earlier.		
6. We'll think more clearly after we get a good night's sleep.		
7. When auditory learners hear words, they remember them better.		
8. Some people speak very quickly.		
9. The test was easy for me because it included a lot of charts and graphs.		
10. Some students listen quietly in class and learn a lot.		
11. I'd rather not come to the lecture today if I can watch it online.		
12. I like to read and listen to a text at the same time.		

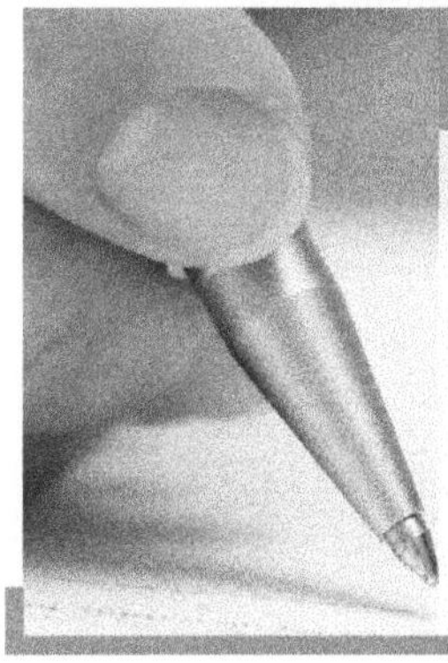

CHECK!

1 A complex sentence is a sentence created by combining an ____________ clause and a dependent clause.

2 Often the dependent clause begins with a subordinating ____________, such as *after*, *because*, *if*, or *when*.

3 Sometimes the independent clause comes first in the sentence, but the dependent clause can also come first. When it does, remember to use a ____________.

C. Practice

1 Read the sentences and add commas where necessary. If no comma is needed, leave it blank.

1 Because John enjoyed building things he wanted to be an engineer.

2 Lee is lucky because he learns well by reading and by listening.

3 After Tiffany figured out that she did not learn easily from lectures she got a library card.

4 If you do not like to read you can listen to podcasts or audiobooks instead.

5 I want to go out with my friends after I finish studying.

6 When my teacher assigns homework I always do it that night.

7 I like studying the textbook after I attend lectures.

8 If I need help I call a friend.

9 Jackson always does better after studying in a group.

10 Before my next test I am going to get a tutor.

2 Read the paragraph. How many complex sentences are there?

[1]Our teacher asked about our learning styles. [2]I thought carefully about how I learn. [3]I am not very good at understanding maps. [4]I do not like classes when I have to read a lot. [5]I remember everything after I go to a lecture. [6]If I know teachers are good lecturers, I take their classes. [7]I cannot build things. [8]I really learn best from listening. [9]After I thought about the way I usually learn, I realized I was an auditory learner.

There are ___ complex sentences. Sentences: ___________

3 Rewrite the sentences putting the independent clause first.

1 After my lectures, I always read through my notes to help me learn them.

____

2 Because I like learning while doing, I decided to train to be a nurse.

____

3 When I am a teacher, I want to understand my students' learning styles.

____

4 After I take my exams, I usually research the things I didn't know.

____

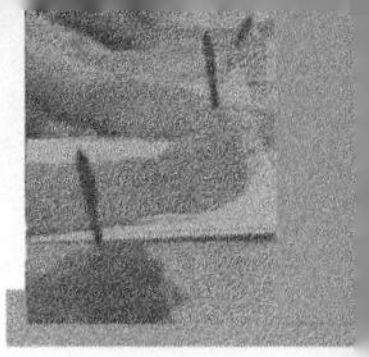

D. Skill Quiz

Check (✓) the correct answer for each item.

1 A simple sentence has ___ dependent clause(s).

- ☐ a. one
- ☐ b. no
- ☐ c. two

2 A simple sentence has ___ independent clause(s).

- ☐ a. two
- ☐ b. no
- ☐ c. one

3 A dependent clause does not express a

- ☐ a. complete idea.
- ☐ b. complete phrase.
- ☐ c. verb.

4 A dependent clause must be combined with an ___ to make a complete sentence.

- ☐ a. independent clause
- ☐ b. independent thought
- ☐ c. adjective

5 Dependent clauses often begin with a subordinating

- ☐ a. subject.
- ☐ b. preposition.
- ☐ c. conjunction.

6 You must use a comma after the dependent clause when the dependent clause comes ___ the independent clause.

- ☐ a. after
- ☐ b. before
- ☐ c. into

7 Choose the independent clause.

- ☐ a. I did not study for the test.
- ☐ b. Before I took the test.
- ☐ c. If I get a good grade in my math class.

8 Choose the dependent clause.

- ☐ a. Before they understood the importance of learning styles.
- ☐ b. She is an auditory learner.
- ☐ c. They each have a different learning style.

9 Choose the complex sentence.

- ☐ a. Mitch and Eddie did not like the movie about robots.
- ☐ b. When they were watching the movie, they yawned a lot.
- ☐ c. They did not stay for the whole thing.

10 Which sentence needs a comma?

- ☐ a. You will understand better after you read the book.
- ☐ b. I ask questions when I do not understand.
- ☐ c. Because he is a kinesthetic learner he likes to work with his hands.

15

Sentence Combining for Variety

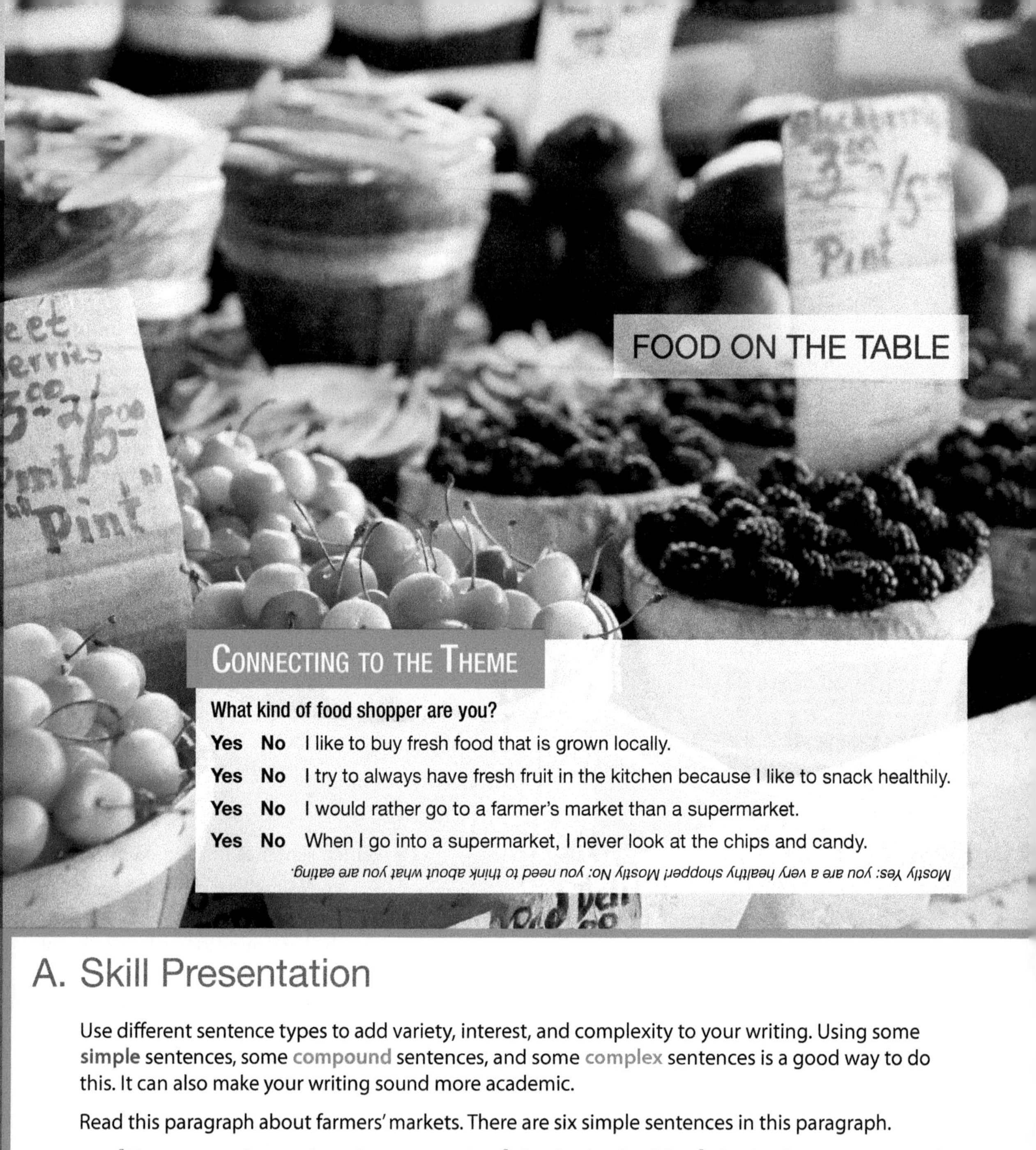

FOOD ON THE TABLE

Connecting to the Theme

What kind of food shopper are you?

Yes **No** I like to buy fresh food that is grown locally.

Yes **No** I try to always have fresh fruit in the kitchen because I like to snack healthily.

Yes **No** I would rather go to a farmer's market than a supermarket.

Yes **No** When I go into a supermarket, I never look at the chips and candy.

Mostly Yes: you are a very healthy shopper! Mostly No: you need to think about what you are eating.

A. Skill Presentation

Use different sentence types to add variety, interest, and complexity to your writing. Using some **simple** sentences, some **compound** sentences, and some **complex** sentences is a good way to do this. It can also make your writing sound more academic.

Read this paragraph about farmers' markets. There are six simple sentences in this paragraph.

> [S]Shopping at farmers' markets is popular. [S]The food is healthy. [S]The food is not processed. [S]There are usually no chemicals. [S]Many people shop at local markets now. [S]More people will buy food from them in the future.

Now read this paragraph.

> [CX]Shopping at farmers' markets is popular because the food is healthy. [CM]The food is not processed, so there are usually no chemicals. [CM]Many people shop at local markets now, and more people will buy food from them in the future.

Now there are only three sentences in the paragraph. The writer combined sentences to add variety to the paragraph. There is now one complex sentence (an independent clause combined with a dependent clause) and two compound sentences (an independent clause combined with a second independent clause). This paragraph is more interesting to read.

B. Over to You

1 Check (✓) the paragraph that has more sentence variety.

☐ **1** Farmers' markets are good for the environment. People can buy only what they need. They do not waste as much. Farmers do not transport their foods a long way. This saves gasoline.

☐ **2** Farmers' markets are good for the environment. People can buy only what they need, so they do not waste as much. Farmers do not transport their foods a long way, which saves gasoline.

2 Read the paragraph and answer the questions

[1]Farmers' markets are becoming more popular, but they have both advantages and disadvantages. [2]One advantage is the fresh food. [3]Some people like farmers' markets because they can talk directly to farmers. [4]Farmers usually sell many kinds of fruits and vegetables. [5]One disadvantage of farmers' markets is the cost. [6]The food is often more expensive, and some people do not think it is worth the high price. [7]Packaged foods are not sold at farmers' markets, so people still have to go to the store to find these items. [8]Also, most farmers' markets are open only one day a week.

1 How many simple sentences does the paragraph have? ______ Sentences: ___________

2 How many compound sentences does the paragraph have? ______ Sentences: ___________

3 How many complex sentences does the paragraph have? ______ Sentences: ___________

4 What conjunctions are used? ______________________

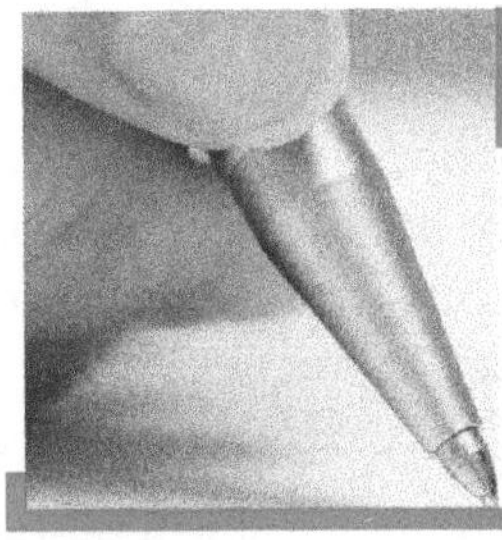

CHECK!

1 When you write paragraphs, use some simple sentences, some compound sentences, and some ___________ sentences.

2 Using different ___________ types adds variety and complexity.

3 It can make your writing more ___________.

C. Practice

1 Read each sentence in the chart. Decide whether it is simple, compound, or complex. Check (✓) the box in the correct column.

	SIMPLE	COMPOUND	COMPLEX
1. Although the supermarket is closer, Talia shopped at the farmers' market.			
2. The local market has all the ingredients she needs, and it has fresh food.			
3. Food at her local store is not as fresh.			
4. She does not want vegetables in packages, and she does not want food from a warehouse.			
5. Talia wants her food to be healthy.			
6. Because chemicals are used on some vegetables, she thinks they are less healthy.			
7. Talia does not buy too much food.			
8. She will serve a healthy meal, and she will use only local ingredients.			

2 Check (✓) the paragraph with the most sentence variety.

☐ **1** Many people want to know where their food comes from. It is difficult to know for sure, but a few things are clear. Much of our food is transported long distances before it arrives at a processing plant. Several things happen next. Before the food is packaged, chemicals are sometimes added. After it leaves the plant, food sometimes sits in a warehouse. It is then distributed to a supermarket, or it is taken to other food stores. Finally, people buy the food, and its journey is over.

☐ **2** There is a special international students' dinner every year at Loudon College. The students each pay $5. Most students think the fresh food is worth more. The food all comes from the farmers' market near school. There is always a big salad with lettuce, tomatoes, and onions. None of these vegetables are wasted. Professor Suarez distributes food to all the international students. Everyone feels healthy at the end of the dinner.

☐ **3** The supermarket is close, but Talia shops at the farmers' market. The local market has all the ingredients she needs, and it has fresh food. She still buys some food at the supermarket, but she does not want any toxic chemicals in her food. Talia wants her food to be healthy, and she thinks chemicals are less healthy. She will cook a healthy meal tonight, and she will use fresh local ingredients.

D. Skill Quiz

Check (✓) the correct answer for each item.

1 One independent clause is a ___ sentence.

- a. simple
- b. compound
- c. complex

2 Combining two independent clauses creates a ___ sentence.

- a. simple
- b. compound
- c. complex

3 A ___ sentence has an independent clause and a dependent clause.

- a. compound
- b. simple
- c. complex

4 Combining sentences can make your writing

- a. easy to grade.
- b. perfect.
- c. more interesting.

5 *I enjoy the farmers' market because it has fresh food and a good selection.*
This is a ___ sentence.

- a. simple
- b. complex
- c. compound

6 *Food at supermarkets is often transported far, and it is packaged.*
This is a ___ sentence.

- a. compound
- b. simple
- c. complex

7 *I went to the supermarket before I went to the farmers' market.*
This is a complex sentence because it has

- a. a coordinating conjunction.
- b. a dependent clause.
- c. two independent clauses.

8 *The farmers' market is a good way to buy fresh and tasty food.*
This is a simple sentence because it has one

- a. independent clause.
- b. dependent clause.
- c. coordinating conjunction.

9 Complete this complex sentence: *I go to the farmers' market ___ I go to the supermarket.*

- a. and
- b. before
- c. but

10 Complete this compound sentence: *Max has not been to the market downtown, ___ he has been to the one near school.*

- a. because
- b. after
- c. but

LIFE LISTS

Connecting to the Theme

Do you have clear short- and long-term goals? The timeframe for short-term goals is a day, a week, or a month. Long-term goals are things that you plan to achieve later, for example, in a year or a lifetime.

A I make a to-do list every day and stick to it.	**B** I don't like lists. I take each day as it comes.
A I study for two hours every morning.	**B** I study whenever I can.
A I'm going to be an accountant.	**B** I'm not sure what career I want to have.
A I'd like to have two children and a dog.	**B** I don't know if I want to have children or pets.
A I want to pay off my student loans when I'm thirty.	**B** I'll pay off my student loans when I can.

Mostly As: you have clear goals! You like to plan ahead and you don't like surprises.
Mostly Bs: you don't have clear goals. You go where life takes you.

A. Skill Presentation

A **general statement** is not specific. It is broad and does not give details. General statements often contain quantifiers such as *many*, *much*, and *a lot*.

> Sheila has many long-term career goals.

This is a general statement. We do not know exactly how many long-term goals Sheila has. We also do not know exactly what her career goals are.

It is important to be specific when you write. Include **specific examples** to make your writing clearer and more interesting. Specific examples often include precise details, numbers, and facts.

> ^{G}Jorge has many short-term goals for school. ^{S}He plans to find a tutor, to study 30 minutes a day, and to score 90 percent on his next English test.

The first sentence is a general statement. The second sentence gives specific examples. It describes three of Jorge's specific short-term goals: *to find a tutor, to study 30 minutes a day,* and *to score 90 percent on his next English test.*

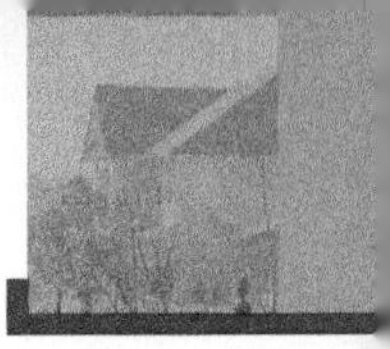

B. Over to You

1 Read the sentences and underline the specific examples. How many specific examples are there?

1 [1]I have many study goals. [2]I want to finish my first degree, study for my masters overseas, and get a research position at a top university.

There is/are ___ specific example(s). They are in sentence ___.

2 [1]Get a part-time job and be careful how you spend your money. [2]There are many ways to save money.

There is/are ___ specific example(s). They are in sentence ___.

2 Match each general statement (1–8) with the correct specific example (a–h).

___ **1** There are many things we can do to help the environment.

___ **2** The students in my class hope to do better next semester.

___ **3** Learning to play a musical instrument is a good long-term goal.

___ **4** Max is planning to eat better.

___ **5** Preparing for a marathon involves a lot of hard work.

___ **6** Aysun and I are proud of our many academic accomplishments.

___ **7** Experts say it is important to set many goals.

___ **8** I love listening to live music.

a It requires proper equipment, motivation, and at least eight months of training.

b They claim that setting realistic long-term goals helps people stay motivated and achieve new things.

c He will enroll in cooking classes, buy vegetarian cookbooks, and start making his own meals.

d They can do this by finding tutors, studying every day, and participating in class.

e We can reduce pollution, develop alternative energy sources, and cut down fewer trees.

f Studies show that playing the violin for an hour each week can increase your ability to learn other things.

g I am planning to go to three jazz recitals and two rock concerts this summer.

h For example, we learned to speak Chinese, and we got As on our final project.

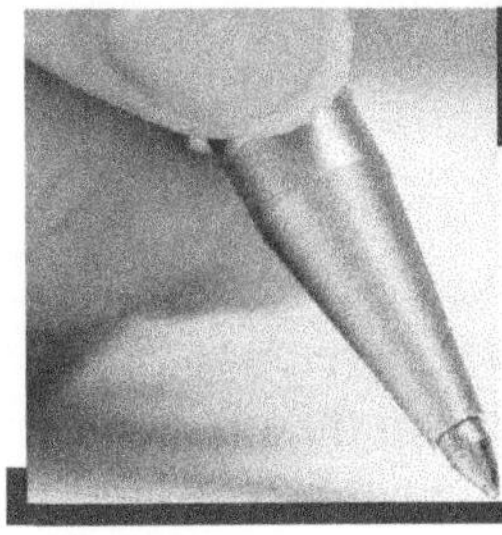

CHECK!

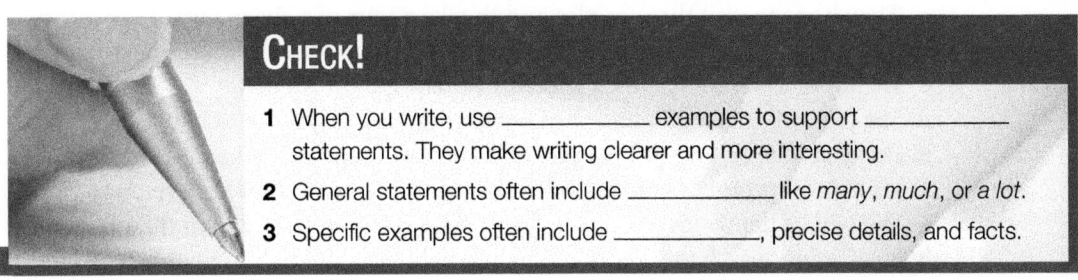

1 When you write, use ___________ examples to support ___________ statements. They make writing clearer and more interesting.

2 General statements often include ___________ like *many*, *much*, or *a lot*.

3 Specific examples often include ___________, precise details, and facts.

C. Practice

1 Read each sentence in the chart. Decide whether it is a general statement or a sentence with specific examples. Check (✓) the box in the correct column.

	GENERAL STATEMENT	SENTENCE WITH SPECIFIC EXAMPLES
1. Carla has many long-term social goals.		
2. Carla hopes to learn to paint and to volunteer at a clinic this year.		
3. I'd like to travel a lot in my life.		
4. I plan to visit Buenos Aires, Johannesburg, and Berlin in the next two years.		
5. My short-term academic goals are to study an hour each day and to get As and Bs on my tests.		
6. Sheila plans to start many hobbies.		
7. Sheila hopes to learn to knit and to paint.		
8. A lot of people study languages.		
9. My goals for the next five years are to buy a house, get married, and have two children.		
10. Carlo loves to eat.		

2 Match each general statement (1–8) with the correct specific example (a–h).

___ **1** Sheila has a lot of goals for spending her money.

___ **2** Ana needs to do some research for her trip to Italy.

___ **3** I hope to have many travel adventures in my lifetime.

___ **4** Jeff has a lot of accomplishments.

___ **5** Karl is motivated to achieve his short-term fitness goals.

___ **6** Meg and Stefan have realistic plans for their trip to Scotland.

___ **7** I have some short-term goals that will help me graduate from college soon.

___ **8** My mother has many hopes for me.

a They hope to visit three castles and to take a tour of a sheep farm.
b I plan to talk to my adviser tomorrow and sign up for two classes next week.
c He hopes to lose 15 pounds and run a marathon in August.
d She plans to invest 25 percent of her savings and buy a home.
e For example, I'd love to bike across France and tour the rainforest in Costa Rica.
f He is most proud of graduating in the top 10 percent of his college class.
g She will be happy if I get married and have children before I am thirty.
h She should search the Internet, buy travel books, and talk to people who have been there.

D. Skill Quiz

Check (✓) the correct answer for each item.

1 A general statement

- a. is broad and not specific.
- b. contains several specific examples.
- c. lists precise facts.

2 In which type of sentence are the quantifiers *many*, *much*, and *a lot* often found?

- a. specific sentences
- b. general sentences
- c. precise sentences

3 Specific examples

- a. often include precise details, numbers, and facts.
- b. often include quantifiers such as *many*, *much*, and *a lot*.
- c. are often broad.

4 Specific examples make writing

- a. broad and not specific.
- b. confusing and unclear.
- c. interesting and clear.

5 Choose the general statement.

- a. Sarah earns 50 percent more now than she did two years ago.
- b. Sarah hopes to receive a pay increase of $200 per month.
- c. Sarah has many long-term career goals.

6 Choose the sentence with specific examples.

- a. Josef loves to fish, play racquetball, and read.
- b. Josef has a lot of hobbies.
- c. Josef enjoys many different activities.

7 Choose the specific sentence that best matches this general statement: *We have many plans for the summer.*

- a. We hope to have a lot of fun.
- b. We plan to barbecue every night, to learn to play tennis, and to visit the beach.
- c. Our long-term goals are to travel, to learn to speak Italian, and to travel to Italy in two years.

8 Choose the specific sentence that best matches this general statement: *Jamie needs to set academic goals.*

- a. He should study a lot.
- b. He should save money.
- c. He should find a study group, work with a tutor, and spend more time on his homework.

9 Choose the general statement that best matches this specific sentence: *For example, they could exercise three times a week and eat vegetables every day.*

- a. Xui Li and Marisa should set learning goals.
- b. Xui Li and Marisa should set health goals.
- c. Xui Li and Marisa should set travel goals.

10 Choose the general statement that best matches this specific sentence: *He must choose whether he wants to study Japanese, Russian, or French and then sign up for classes.*

- a. Angel wants to learn a new language.
- b. Angel has many goals for the weekend.
- c. Angel has a lot of free time.

17

Punctuation 2: More About Commas

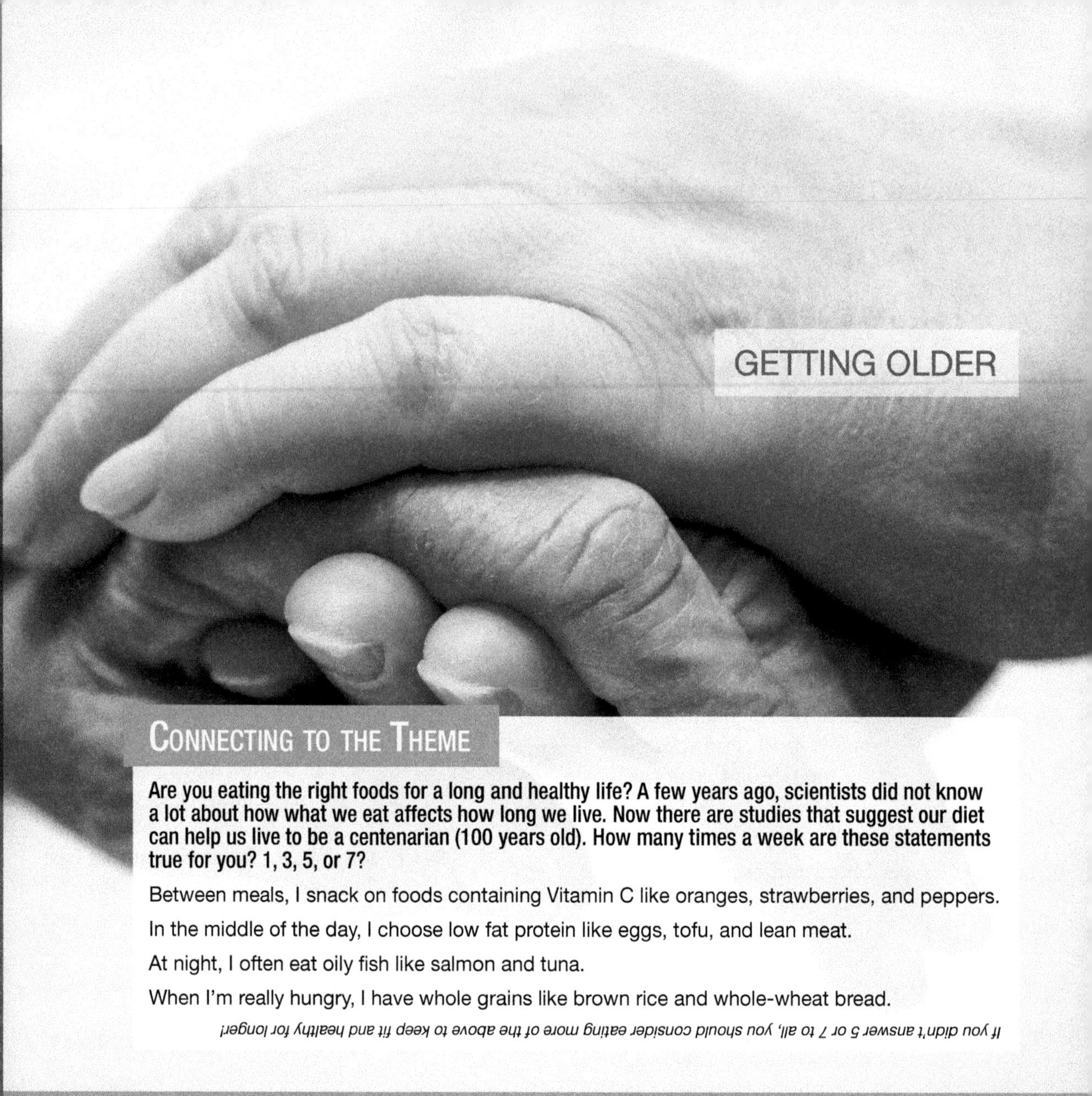

GETTING OLDER

Connecting to the Theme

Are you eating the right foods for a long and healthy life? A few years ago, scientists did not know a lot about how what we eat affects how long we live. Now there are studies that suggest our diet can help us live to be a centenarian (100 years old). How many times a week are these statements true for you? 1, 3, 5, or 7?

Between meals, I snack on foods containing Vitamin C like oranges, strawberries, and peppers.

In the middle of the day, I choose low fat protein like eggs, tofu, and lean meat.

At night, I often eat oily fish like salmon and tuna.

When I'm really hungry, I have whole grains like brown rice and whole-wheat bread.

If you didn't answer 5 or 7 to all, you should consider eating more of the above to keep fit and healthy for longer!

A. Skill Presentation

Commas are used between clause and to separate items in lists. However, commas are also used to separate **time clauses**, **time expressions**, and **transition words** from the rest of a sentence. This is only true when the phrases occur before the clause they describe.

Read the following examples.

Before they participated in the study, all the monkeys ate what they wanted.

There is a comma after the time clause at the beginning of the sentence.

In the beginning, researchers divided the monkeys into two groups.

There is a comma after the time expression at the beginning of this sentence.

Finally, the monkeys who ate less lived longer.

There is a comma after the transition word at the beginning of this sentence.

B. Over to You

1 Read the sentences and add commas where necessary. If no comma is needed, leave it blank.

1 The researchers were excited after the study ended successfully.

2 Lastly the monkeys who ate less were healthier.

3 Before the study the researchers didn't know what to expect.

4 The researchers finished writing their reports in June 2012.

5 Until the study ended the researchers could not talk about their discoveries.

6 In the end they learned a lot about aging from the monkeys.

2 Read each sentence in the chart. Decide if the comma is in the correct place or not. Check (✓) the box in the correct column.

	CORRECT PLACE	INCORRECT PLACE
1. When we go on our trip, we should try to eat fewer calories.		
2. Before, we go home I want to exercise more.		
3. When she was 100 years old, my grandmother shared her secrets for a long life.		
4. After I decided, to increase my life span I began eating less sugar.		
5. After dinner, we will take a walk.		
6. Ms. Lopez supported her son until, he got a job on campus.		
7. Before David started his diet, he felt tired and unhealthy.		
8. After cancer treatment Tom ate less, and exercised more.		
9. Before the state, offered special food services the city did not have any.		
10. Finally, researchers know more about living longer.		

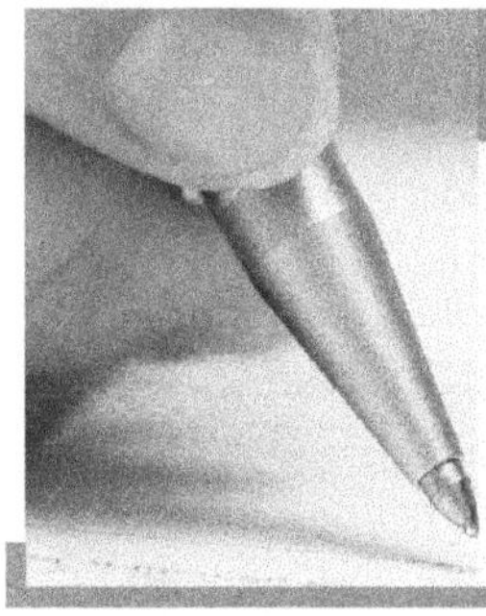

CHECK!

1 Use a comma to separate the following from the rest of the sentence:

a. ____________ ____________, e.g., *before they participated in the study*

b. ____________ ____________, e.g., *in the beginning*

c. ____________ ____________, e.g., *finally*

2 Only use a comma when they come at the ____________ of a sentence.

C. Practice

1 Read the sentences and add commas where necessary. If no comma is needed, leave it blank.

1 Firstly the researchers studied calories and longevity.

2 Her grandmother ate everything she wanted before she started her diet.

3 When people improve their diets they can prevent heart disease.

4 Until the end of his life James only ate fruits and vegetables.

5 After Ms. Lopez lost 50 pounds she felt healthier.

6 After work Andy always tries to go for a long bike ride.

7 Next you need to eat fewer desserts.

8 My grandfather used government services after he realized he needed more support.

9 In the morning some people eat a healthy breakfast.

10 Aunt Sara and Uncle Mike both lived to be 100 in the end.

2 Read the paragraph and add commas where necessary. If no comma is needed, leave it blank.

When[1] researchers studied people who were over 100[2] they discovered some secrets to longevity. What did they learn? When they chose their diets[3] many of these people ate[4] more vegetables than meat. They also tried[5] not to eat too much. These older people took gentle exercise[6] when they were able to. In the end[7] the study found that the centenarians[8] put their families first. When researchers asked[9] what was most important to them[10] the answer was often family and friends.

3 Read the sentences and decide why they have a comma. Write *TE* for Time Expression, *TC* for Time Clause, or *TW* for Transition Word.

___ 1 When I go on a hike, I take raisins to snack on.

___ 2 Secondly, they did not know how much salt was in the food.

___ 3 Recently, I learned that oily fish is very good for your skin.

___ 4 In the afternoon, I try not to drink coffee or tea.

___ 5 After a workout, I always eat a high protein snack.

___ 6 Finally, Maria started eating fruit for breakfast and felt much better.

___ 7 This week, I am going to eat a different colored vegetable every day.

___ 8 Lastly, try to drink plenty of water during the day.

___ 9 Before I knew about eating healthily, I used to eat lots of junk food.

___ 10 At night, I usually take a glass of water to bed.

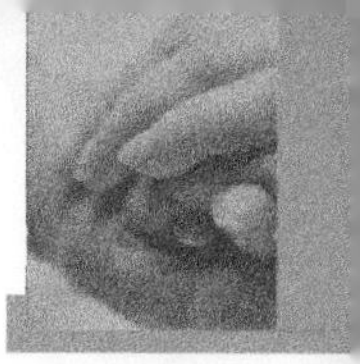

D. Skill Quiz

Check (✓) the correct answer for each item.

1 Use a comma to separate a time clause that is

☐ a. at the end of the sentence.
☐ b. at the beginning of the sentence.
☐ c. not connected to the sentence.

2 *My aunt was always very tired, before she lost 40 pounds.*
Is the comma in the correct place in this sentence?

☐ a. No. This sentences does not need a comma.
☐ b. Yes. The comma is in the correct place.
☐ c. No. It should come after the word *before.*

3 *When older, people become less independent they should spend more time with family.*
Is the comma in the correct place in this sentence?

☐ a. No. This sentence does not need a comma.
☐ b. Yes. The comma is in the correct place.
☐ c. No. It should come after the word *independent.*

4 *In the beginning the monkeys were divided into two groups.*
Where should a comma go in this sentence?

☐ a. after the word *in*
☐ b. after the word *beginning*
☐ c. after the word *two*

5 *When they ate less they felt healthier.*
Where should a comma go in this sentence?

☐ a. after the word *less*
☐ b. after the word *when*
☐ c. after the word *felt*

6 *When they chose their food the centenarians ate more vegetables.*
Where should a comma go in this sentence?

☐ a. after the word *centenarians*
☐ b. after the word *when*
☐ c. after the word *food*

7 *Before he goes to work Ben likes to exercise for an hour.*
Where should the comma go in this sentence?

☐ a. after the word *before*
☐ b. after the word *work*
☐ c. after the word *exercise*

8 Which sentence has the comma in the correct place?

☐ a. Secondly Grace should go to the gym, three times a week.
☐ b. Secondly Grace should go, to the gym three times a week.
☐ c. Secondly, Grace should go to the gym three times a week.

9 Which sentence has the comma in the correct place?

☐ a. In the end, we know more about living longer.
☐ b. Carol took a short walk around the park, in the evening.
☐ c. Before you stop working it is important to know, about government services.

10 *In the next year the researcher will write a report about how centenarians live longer.*
How many commas does this sentence need?

☐ a. none
☐ b. one
☐ c. two

18

Capitalization Rules 2

LEARNING TO COMMUNICATE

Connecting to the Theme

The National Association of Colleges and Employers (NACE) has made a list of the skills that employers look for in their employees. These are the five skills that top the list. How would you rank them?

___ technical skills (able to do particular tasks)

___ analytical skills (able to understand problems and solve them)

___ communication skills

___ ability to work as part of a team

___ willingness to work hard

Actual ranking according to NACE: 1 communication skills, 2 analytical skills, 3 teamwork, 4 technical skills, 5 willing to work hard.

A. Skill Presentation

In English, it's important to know when to use capital letters. Proper nouns are always capitalized:

PEOPLE: Laura Bridgman **PLACES:** Nicaragua
THINGS: the White House **ORGANIZATIONS:** Perkins School for the Blind

Follow these four rules of capitalization:

1 Always capitalize course names, for example, *Business Administration and Intermediate Grammar.*

2 Always capitalize titles of publications, including books, magazines, newspapers, and even online journals. In titles with multiple words, most of the words are capitalized. "Little" words, like *and*, *the*, and *a*, are not capitalized unless they come first. For example, in the title *Skills for Effective Writing*, capitalize *skills*, *effective*, and *writing*. Do not capitalize the word *for*.

3 Always capitalize days of the week, months of the year, and holidays. Do not capitalize the seasons *spring*, *summer*, *fall*, or *winter*. For example, the words *Friday*, *November*, and *Mother's Day* are all capitalized.

4 Always capitalize geographic areas. This includes continents, regions, countries, cities, and states. For example, *the United States*, *the Midwest*, and *Detroit*, *Michigan* are all capitalized.

B. Over to You

1 Circle the letters that should be capitalized.

1 I'm taking psychology and language development this semester.

2 Did you see the article about language learning in the washington post? It reminded me of something I read on yahoo news.

3 In july, I took an interesting course. Classes met monday and wednesday, but not on independence day.

4 I read an article about the languages of brazil and other countries in south america.

2 Circle the correct forms of the words.

1 The university is offering several interesting zoology courses this *September* | *september*.

2 One course in particular, *Animal Language* | *animal language*, explores the ways animals communicate.

3 The professor typically lectures about topics like *politics and language* | *Politics and Language*.

4 For their final project, students research different kinds of *animal communication* | *Animal Communication*.

5 In this course, you will read the book *Animal Communication* | *animal communication* by Anne Somerset.

6 The course meets on *Mondays and Wednesdays* | *mondays and wednesdays*.

7 The final exam will be on *August* | *august* 24.

8 Students must take the course *Human Social Behavior* | *human social behavior* before they can register for this course.

9 Please note that the course will not meet on *Independence Day* | *independence day*.

10 Registration starts the *last week of May* | *Last Week of May*.

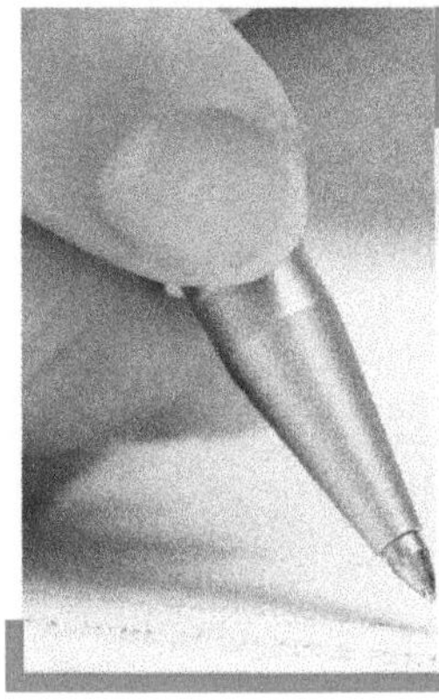

CHECK!

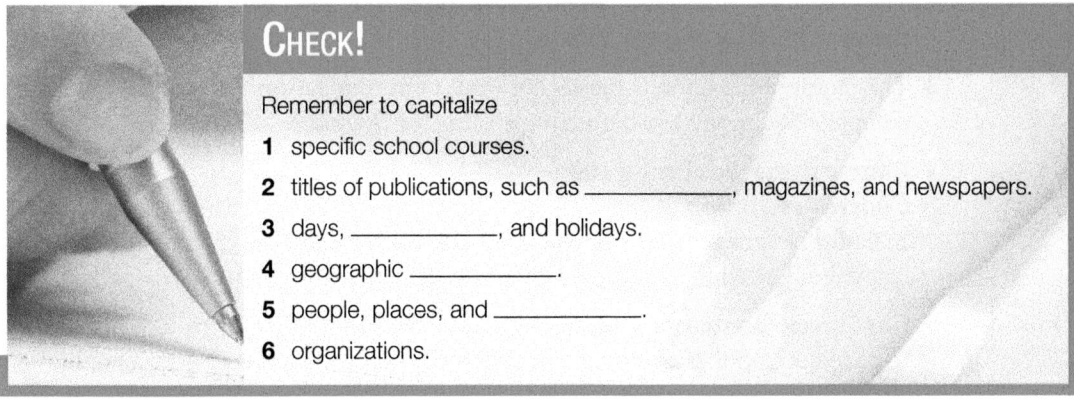

Remember to capitalize

1 specific school courses.

2 titles of publications, such as ____________, magazines, and newspapers.

3 days, ____________, and holidays.

4 geographic ____________.

5 people, places, and ____________.

6 organizations.

C. Practice

1 Circle the letters that should be capitalized.

To:	Foundations of Language students
Subject:	Course information
From:	Professor Collings

Welcome!
This course is called [1][f]oundations of [2][l]anguage. We will explore typical [3][l]anguage [4][d]evelopment in the children of [5][n]orth [6][a]merica.
Your main textbook is *[7][f]irst [8][l]anguage [9][a]cquisition*. It will help answer some important questions:
How do babies [10][c]ommunicate before they learn [11][l]anguage?
At what [12][a]ge do they form their first [13][w]ords?
Then, we will discuss sign [14][l]anguage from [15][n]icaragua, languages from [16][a]frica, and variations on dialects in the [17][u]nited [18][s]tates.
The two required [19][t]extbooks for this course are *[20][l]earning [21][s]peech* and *The [22][d]evelopment [23][o]f New [24][l]anguage.*
The course will meet on [25][w]ednesdays and [26][f]ridays during the [27][s]pring term, [28][j]anuary to [29][j]une. We will not meet on [30][m]emorial [31][d]ay.

[32][p]rofessor [33][c]ollings

2 Read the course descriptions and circle the words that should be capitalized.

1 **Course name: Sociology 135**
Course description:
work communication is a course about social issues. You will learn how gender affects communication in school and in the workplace.

2 The class meets tuesdays, January 23 through may 18. There is also a lab that meets on the last Thursday of every month.

3 The required textbook is mastering work communication. All students must first complete Sociology 130 before registering for this class.

4 **Course name: Education 102**
Course description:
In Child Language Development, you will learn about how children normally learn language. The course requires a school visit in the chicago area.

5 Class meets Tuesdays and thursdays in the fall, September 2 through december 3. The required textbook is *Child Language Development*. This class is four credits.

D. Skill Quiz

Check (✓) the correct answer for each item.

1 Always capitalize ___ because they are proper nouns.

- ☐ a. school supplies
- ☐ b. grade levels
- ☐ c. specific school courses

2 Always capitalize ___ because they are proper nouns.

- ☐ a. times of the day
- ☐ b. months of the year
- ☐ c. seasons

3 Always capitalize ___ because they are proper nouns.

- ☐ a. names of plants
- ☐ b. names of cities
- ☐ c. directions

4 In the title of a publication, you should usually capitalize

- ☐ a. most words.
- ☐ b. only the "little" words.
- ☐ c. none of the words.

5 *The course meets every tuesday during the summer.*
Which word should be capitalized in this sentence?

- ☐ a. course
- ☐ b. tuesday
- ☐ c. summer

6 *I got a good grade in writing 101.*
Which word should be capitalized in this sentence?

- ☐ a. good
- ☐ b. grade
- ☐ c. writing

7 *I am taking an interesting course this semester called animal communication.*
Which words should be capitalized in this sentence?

- ☐ a. interesting and course
- ☐ b. this and semester
- ☐ c. animal and communication

8 *After new year's, the next semester at my college begins.*
Which words should be capitalized in this sentence?

- ☐ a. new and year's
- ☐ b. next and semester
- ☐ c. my and college

9 *You will read articles from the journal language in society.*
Which words should be capitalized in this sentence?

- ☐ a. will and read
- ☐ b. the and journal
- ☐ c. language and society

10 *The textbook language development has good information about how children become literate.*
Which words should be capitalized in this sentence?

- ☐ a. language and development
- ☐ b. good and information
- ☐ c. children and literate

19

Transition Words 1: Chronological Order

AMAZING SCIENCE

Connecting to the Theme

Do you know what a camera pill is? How do you think it works? Choose the correct set of steps.

A A camera pill is a tiny camera that looks like a pill. The doctor looks at pictures on his computer. The tiny camera takes lots of pictures as it travels through the body. The patient swallows the camera pill.

B A camera pill is a tiny camera that looks like a pill. It is so small that it can be swallowed by patients. First, the patient swallows the camera pill. Then, the tiny camera takes lots of pictures as it travels through the body. Finally, the doctor looks at the pictures on his computer.

The correct set of steps is B.

A. Skill Presentation

Transition words are words that show connections between ideas. They help ideas in a paragraph make sense. Transition words are very important in writing.

Chronological order is the order in which events happen in time. When you write about the steps in a process, it's important that the chronological order is clear. There are several transition words that show chronological order. They show the reader the order in which the steps happen.

Look at this chart showing transition words you can use to show the first step, additional steps, and the last step of a process.

First step	Additional steps	Last step
first	second	finally
to start	third	lastly
	then	
	after that	
	next	

When you write, put a comma after most transition words.

First, the doctor looks at the images.

After that, the pictures are sent to a computer.

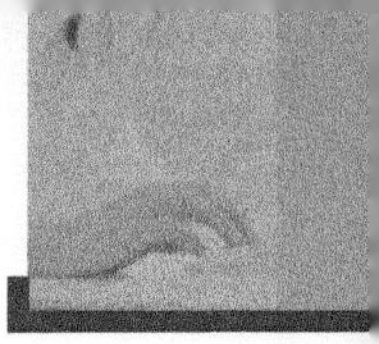

B. Over to You

1 Circle the correct transition words in the steps for having an x-ray.

[1]*Finally,* | *Next,* | *First,* the nurse explains the reason for the x-ray. [2]*After that,* | *To start,* | *Finally,* the patient lies down on the table. [3]*First,* | *Lastly,* | *Then,* the x-ray machine takes the picture. [4]*Finally,* | *Second,* | *First,* the doctor looks at the images.

2 Look at each step in the chart and decide if it is a first step, an additional step, or a last step. Check (✓) the box in the correct column.

	FIRST STEP	ADDITIONAL STEPS	LAST STEP
1. Then, ask a doctor for help.			
2. First, call your doctor.			
3. Lastly, look at the results.			
4. After that, add batteries.			
5. To start, get an x-ray.			
6. Next, look at the sensor.			
7. Second, take two pills.			
8. Finally, put the top back on.			
9. To begin, open the bottle.			
10. Third, test your balance.			
11. Then, pick up the camera.			
12. Lastly, take the x-rays to your doctor.			

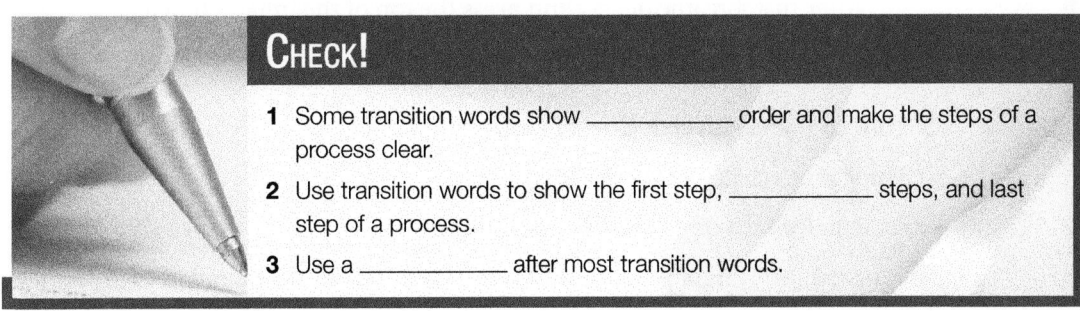

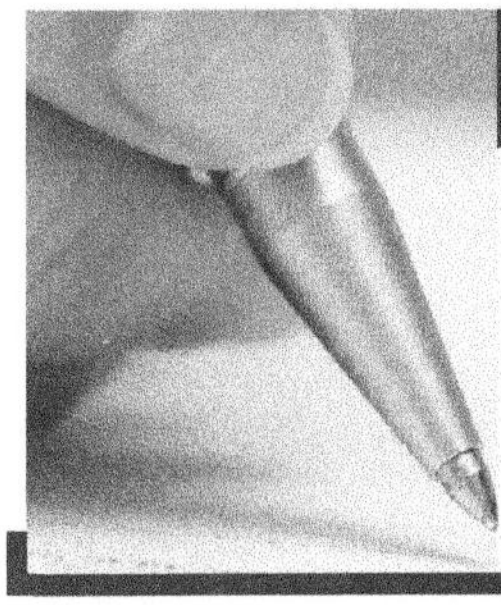

CHECK!

1 Some transition words show ____________ order and make the steps of a process clear.

2 Use transition words to show the first step, ____________ steps, and last step of a process.

3 Use a ____________ after most transition words.

C. Practice

1 Read the paragraph about medicine patches. How many transition words show chronological order?

[1]Recently, a company invented a new patch. [2]The patch contains medicine. [3]Surprisingly, it is easy to use. [4]To begin, you need to get a prescription. [5]Next, get the patch at a local pharmacy. [6]Then you put the patch on your skin. [7]After that, you leave it alone. [8]The patch has small needles on it. [9]These needles go into the skin, and the medicine goes into the body. [10]Fortunately, the needles do not hurt. [11]Finally, you take off the patch. [12]Especially for older people, this invention is very helpful. [13]With this patch, they don't have to worry about forgetting to take medicine.

There are ___ transition words that show chronological order. Sentences: __________

The transition words used are ____________________.

2 Number the steps in the instructions in the correct chronological order.

1 The Endo-Pat

The Endo-Pat can tell if you are at risk of a heart attack.

___ Third, a machine records the patient's blood flow rate.

___ Second, the doctor places a band around the patient's arm.

___ Finally, the doctor looks at the results.

___ First, a doctor puts two clips on a patient's fingers.

2 How to Use an Asthma Inhaler

If you are diagnosed with asthma, an inhaler can help you breathe.

___ Lastly, replace the cap on the inhaler and rinse your mouth.

___ To start, shake the inhaler for 10 seconds and remove the cap.

___ After that, breathe deeply and press the top of the inhaler down.

___ Next, hold the inhaler in front of your mouth.

3 How to Use an Electric Toothbrush

Using an electric toothbrush is easy.

___ Finally, turn off the toothbrush and rinse it off.

___ Next, apply light pressure and move the toothbrush over all of your teeth.

___ Then put the toothbrush in your mouth and turn it on.

___ To begin, put toothpaste on the toothbrush.

___ After you brush your teeth, move the toothbrush over your gums.

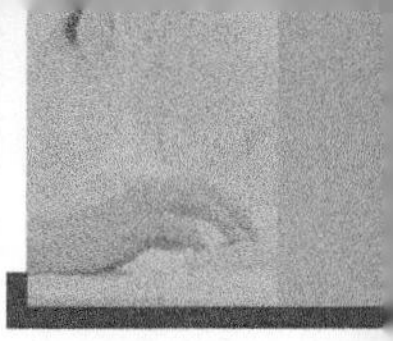

D. Skill Quiz

Check (✓) the correct answer for each item.

1 Transition words

☐ a. only show the first step of a process.
☐ b. connect ideas.
☐ c. describe situations.

2 Chronological order shows

☐ a. the order in which things happen.
☐ b. the order of numbers.
☐ c. the way something looks.

3 Steps of a process can show

☐ a. only the beginning and ending of something.
☐ b. the order of how to do something.
☐ c. how to use transition words.

4 Choose the words that show additional steps of a process.

☐ a. *First*, *To begin*, and *To start*
☐ b. *Lastly* and *Finally*
☐ c. *Second*, *After that*, and *Then*

5 Choose the sentence that shows the first step of a process.

☐ a. Lastly, wait while the doctor takes your x-ray.
☐ b. Next, put the protective cloth on.
☐ c. To begin, stand in front of the camera.

6 Choose the sentence that shows an additional step of a process.

☐ a. First, open your medication.
☐ b. Next, take your medication with water.
☐ c. Finally, put your medication in a safe place.

7 Choose the sentence that shows the last step of a process.

☐ a. To start, go to a doctor.
☐ b. Finally, follow the doctor's instructions.
☐ c. Then get your problem diagnosed.

8 Choose the sentence that has correct punctuation.

☐ a. Third get your prescription filled.
☐ b. Then get your prescription filled.
☐ c. Next get your prescription filled.

9 Choose the sentence that has correct punctuation.

☐ a. After that, look up your results online.
☐ b. After that look up your results online.
☐ c. After, that look up your results online.

10 Choose the steps that are in chronological order.

☐ a. Second, breathe deeply. To start, put the inhaler in your mouth. Lastly, exhale.
☐ b. First, go to a doctor's office. Next, talk to the doctor about your problems. Finally, find out what medication you need to take.
☐ c. To begin, open the package. Finally, take the medication. Then read the instructions.

20

Verb Tense Consistency

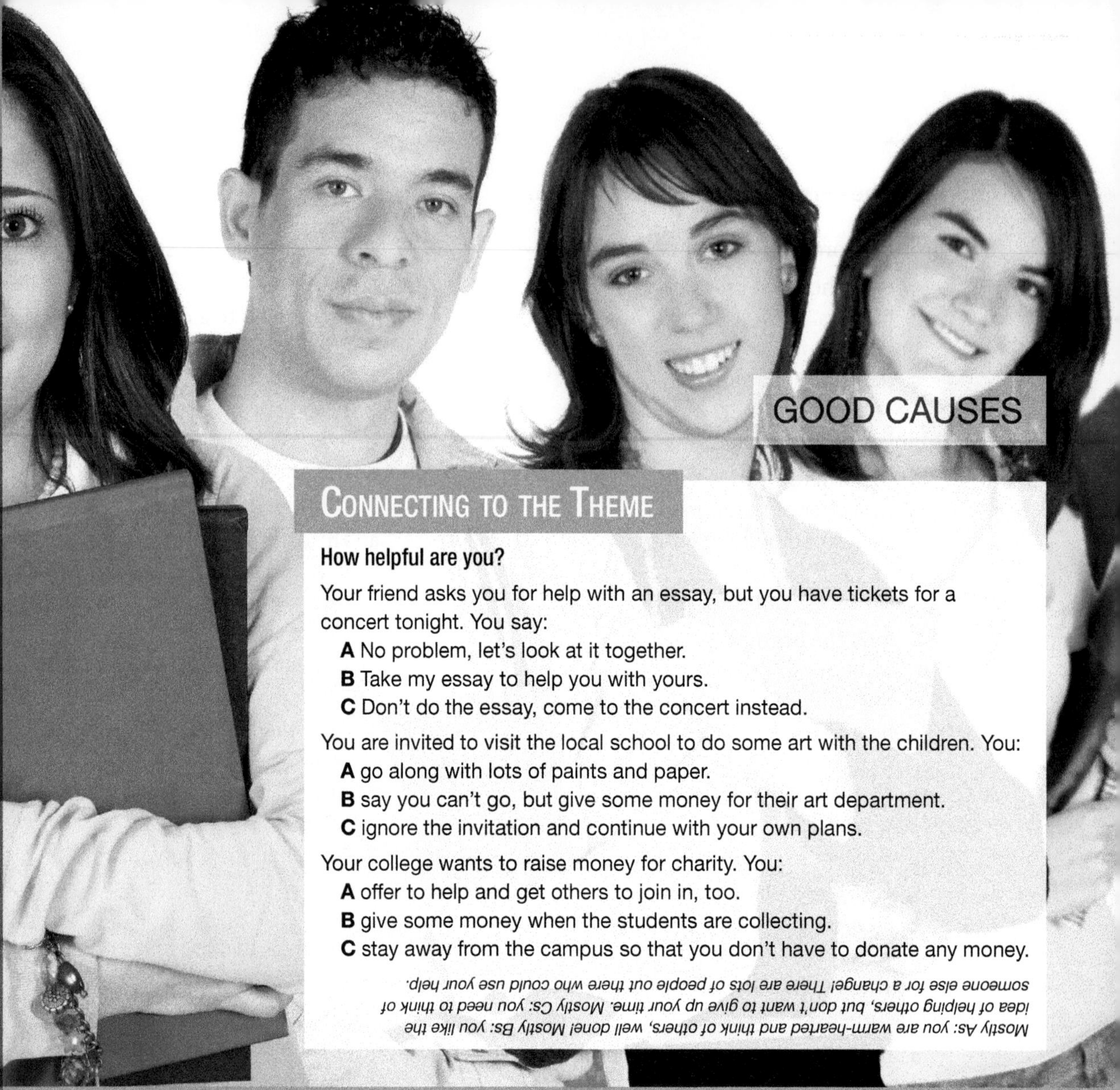

GOOD CAUSES

Connecting to the Theme

How helpful are you?

Your friend asks you for help with an essay, but you have tickets for a concert tonight. You say:

A No problem, let's look at it together.
B Take my essay to help you with yours.
C Don't do the essay, come to the concert instead.

You are invited to visit the local school to do some art with the children. You:

A go along with lots of paints and paper.
B say you can't go, but give some money for their art department.
C ignore the invitation and continue with your own plans.

Your college wants to raise money for charity. You:

A offer to help and get others to join in, too.
B give some money when the students are collecting.
C stay away from the campus so that you don't have to donate any money.

Mostly As: you are warm-hearted and think of others, well done! Mostly Bs: you like the idea of helping others, but don't want to give up your time. Mostly Cs: you need to think of someone else for a change! There are lots of people out there who could use your help.

A. Skill Presentation

It is important to use consistent verb tenses when you write. Using consistent verb tenses helps make your writing clear and easier to understand.

In general, if you begin writing in one tense, you should continue to use the same tense. For example, when you are telling a story in the past tense, do not suddenly switch to the present tense.

After you are finished writing, go back and make sure all the verbs are in the same tense.

> First of all, teachers **benefit** from peer tutoring. Second, peer tutors **make** students more comfortable. Finally, tutors **enjoyed** working with other students. ✗

In this paragraph, the writer made a mistake. In the first two sentences, the verbs *benefit* and *make*, are in the **present tense**. The last verb, *enjoyed*, is in the **past tense**. To make the verb tense consistent, the word *enjoy* should also be in the present tense.

> First of all, teachers **benefit** from peer tutoring. Second, peer tutors **make** students more comfortable. Finally, tutors **enjoy** working with other students. ✓

B. Over to You

1 Underline the verb in bold that is not consistent. Decide what tense it should be in. Write *FUTURE* or *PAST*.

__________ 1 Yesterday, Jin **went** to the elementary school. She **made** art projects with the children. They **paint** together. Jin **had** a great day and so did the children.

__________ 2 Tomorrow, Jin **is going to go** back to the elementary school. She**'s going to teach** the children some recipes. They **make** pizza for the teachers!

2 Read each group of sentences. Which sentences have inconsistent verb tenses? Write the correct verb forms.

1 [1]Stefania and I worked at the clinic last week. [2]People donate blood when we are there. [3]We gave them juice and cookies and made sure they were OK.

The inconsistent verb tenses are in sentence(s) __________.

Correct verb forms: ______________________________

2 [1]Marcus and Ana have many goals this summer. [2]First, they want to work at the homeless shelter. [3]Next, they plan to tutor students in math. [4]Finally, they hoped to get in touch with the mayor and organized more volunteer activities.

The inconsistent verb tenses are in sentence(s) __________.

Correct verb forms: ______________________________

3 [1]Tina and Ray were peer tutors in their English class last semester. [2]They helped their classmates learn many skills. [3]First, they tutor them in writing. [4]Later in the semester, they helped them with grammar. [5]Finally, some students also need help in reading, so Tina and Ray teach them a new skill, too. [6]Tina and Ray like their peer tutoring experience. [7]They developed friendships with their classmates.

The inconsistent verb tenses are in sentence(s) __________.

Correct verb forms: ______________________________

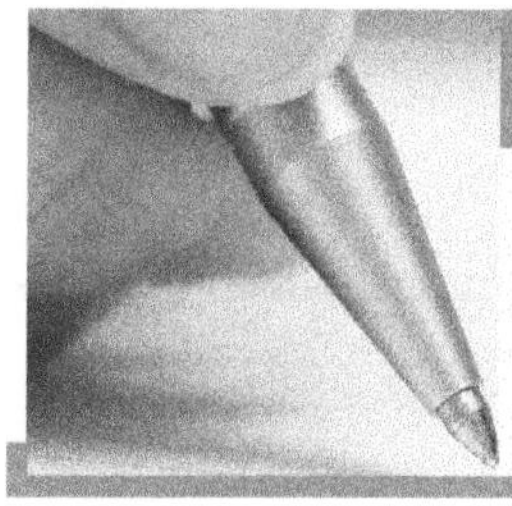

CHECK!

Use consistent verb tenses to make your writing clear and easy to understand. In general, you should start with one tense and continue to use the [1]*different* | *same* tense. Do not change tenses. When you are finished, check your writing to make sure most of the verbs are in [2]*the same* | *a different* tense.

C. Practice

1 Read the paragraphs and look at the verbs in bold. How many of them are not consistent?

1 Peer tutoring, or student-to-student tutoring, can help students who need a hand with their assignments. There **were** many reasons it **is** helpful for students to teach each other. First of all, peer tutoring **helps** teachers. Teachers often **had** large classes. They **did** not always have time to help everyone. Peer tutors **can** give more attention. Second, peer tutors **could** help students feel more comfortable. They may **feel** more relaxed when their tutor **is** a peer. Finally, peer tutoring **was** good for the tutors. Both tutors and the students they help do better on tests. Not surprisingly, peer tutoring **is** a common practice at many colleges.

There are ___ verbs that are not consistent. They are ________________________.

2 I am a peer tutor in my English class this semester. Peer tutoring **helped** my teacher. Our class **is** big, and she **has** problems managing the students. She **did not** always **have** time to work with every student. Peer tutors **give** other students close attention. I **am** good at writing, so I **worked** with my classmates on their writing skills. Their grammar **was** strong, but they **need** help with writing. Now that we **tutor** each other every day, we **got** higher scores on our tests.

There are ___ verbs that are not consistent. They are ________________________.

2 Read the sentences from a paragraph about volunteering. Circle the correct words to make the verbs consistent.

Last summer, I worked as a volunteer in Haiti.

1 I *lived* | *live* | *am going to live* in the countryside and *built* | *build* | *am going to build* houses.

2 I also *will teach* | *teach* | *taught* English to young children.

3 The other volunteers *are* | *were* | *will be* very nice.

4 We *had* | *are having* | *will have* a great time together.

5 My students *are going to be* | *are* | *were* eager to learn English.

6 They *will study* | *study* | *studied* for three hours a day.

7 By the end of the summer, they *speak* | *spoke* | *will speak* very well.

8 I *was* | *am* | *will be* sad to leave the country.

9 However, I *am* | *was* | *am going to be* happy because I *knew* | *know* | *will know* I had helped many people.

D. Skill Quiz

Check (✓) the correct answer for each item.

1 To avoid verb tense inconsistencies, first

☐ a. decide on a tense.
☐ b. check your writing.
☐ c. stay in the past tense.

2 When you have finished writing, check to make sure

☐ a. most verbs are in the present tense.
☐ b. most verbs are in the same tense.
☐ c. most verbs are in the past tense.

3 Using a consistent verb tense helps make your writing

☐ a. harder to understand.
☐ b. longer.
☐ c. clearer.

i. *Our volunteer assignment* ***was*** *to work at the animal shelter.*
ii. *We* ***played*** *with the animals and* ***walked*** *them in the park.*
iii. *Some of the animals* ***are*** *old. They* ***need*** *special medicine.*
iv. *A nice family* ***adopted*** *one of the animals. They* ***gave*** *him a new home.*

4 What describes the verb tenses in the sentences above?

☐ a. The verbs change from the past tense to the present tense, then back to the past tense.
☐ b. The verbs change from the present tense to the past tense.
☐ c. All the verbs are in the same tense.

5 In ii, the correct forms of the verbs are

☐ a. played, walk.
☐ b. played, walked.
☐ c. play, walk.

6 In iii, the correct forms of the verbs are

☐ a. were, need.
☐ b. are, need.
☐ c. were, needed.

7 In iv, the correct forms of the verbs are

☐ a. adopt, give.
☐ b. adopted, give.
☐ c. adopted, gave.

i. *Marcus and Ana* ***worked*** *at the shelter last Saturday. They* ***made*** *soup and salad for dinner.*
ii. *Their teacher* ***asked*** *them to write a report about it. They both* ***wrote*** *essays about their experience.*
iii. *Marcus* ***writes*** *about how he* ***likes*** *meeting people in the community. Ana* ***writes*** *about how she* ***enjoys*** *cooking for people who need food.*

8 Which of the following best describes the reading above?

☐ a. The verbs are all in the past tense.
☐ b. The verbs change from the past tense to the present tense.
☐ c. The verbs change from the present tense to the past tense, then back to the present tense.

9 In i, the correct forms of the verbs are

☐ a. work, make.
☐ b. worked, made.
☐ c. worked, make.

10 In iii, the correct forms of the verb are

☐ a. writes, likes, writes, enjoys.
☐ b. wrote, likes, wrote, enjoys.
☐ c. wrote, liked, wrote, enjoyed.

21

Giving Specific Examples 2

THE RIGHT JOB

Connecting to the Theme

Networking is an extremely important skill nowadays. According to the U.S. Bureau of Labor Statistics, 70% of all jobs are found through networking. What kind of people do you think are good at networking? Rank these five qualities from 1–5, where 1 is the most important.

___ a good talker

___ a careful listener

___ organized

___ confident

___ sociable

Answers will vary.

A. Skill Presentation

It is important to use **specific examples** in your writing. Specific examples give more information about general statements and can make your writing more interesting. Use specific examples to add supporting information.

There are two ways to support **general statements** with specific examples.

1 Use **factual examples**. Factual examples make your idea more specific. Factual examples often include phrases such as *research shows, studies show, according to*, and *experts say*.

[GS]Networking is an important skill. [FE]Research shows that many people find new jobs by networking.

2 Use **descriptive adjectives**. They help support general statements by adding details.

[GS]My boss is an excellent networker. She is **friendly**, **talkative**, and **motivated** to meet new people.

B. Over to You

1 Read the sentences about going on job interviews. Write *FE* for Factual Example or *DA* for Descriptive Adjectives to describe the sentences in bold.

___ 1 You should wear a suit to your interview. **According to experts, candidates who wear suits appear more professional.**

___ 2 I want a job with a good employer. **I would like to work for a large, secure company.**

2 Match each general statement (1–10) with the correct specific example (a–j).

___ 1 It is important to use common sense when dressing for an interview.

___ 2 You can network almost anywhere.

___ 3 Be sure to follow up with new contacts.

___ 4 It is important to assess your positive qualities.

___ 5 Remember to write thank-you notes.

___ 6 Try to relate to people when you are networking.

___ 7 It is possible to interview if you have a full-time job.

___ 8 Some people change careers later in life.

___ 9 Finding a new job requires a positive attitude.

___ 10 When you are job hunting, a good résumé is one of the most important things to have.

a According to *Industry* magazine, every person you meet at an interview should get one.
b Studies show that many employers are happy to interview during off-hours such as evenings or weekends.
c Make sure yours is well-written, clear, and up-to-date.
d Studies show that people who switch careers in their late 40s can be extremely successful.
e Studies show that people who have something in common are more memorable than people who do not.
f Experts say that parties and casual events are good places to meet new people.
g Write them a prompt, thoughtful, and friendly e-mail within 24 hours.
h According to *Career* magazine, you should know what your three best traits are.
i Experts say you must be optimistic and determined to get the job you want.
j Your suit should be clean, conservative, and freshly ironed.

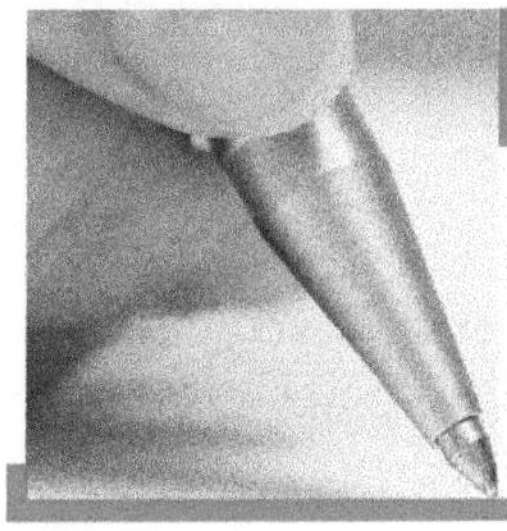

CHECK!

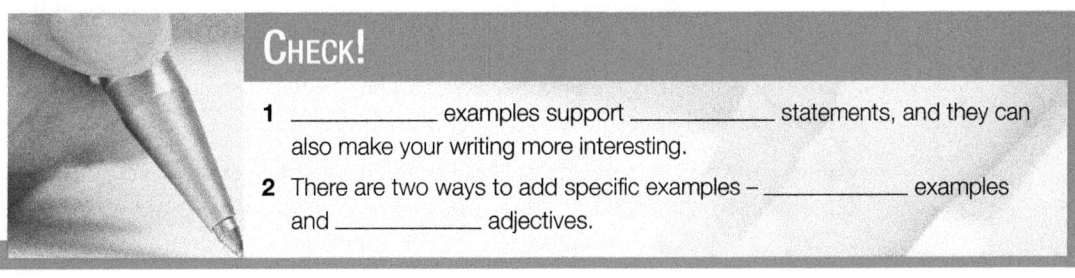

1 ___________ examples support ___________ statements, and they can also make your writing more interesting.

2 There are two ways to add specific examples – ___________ examples and ___________ adjectives.

C. Practice

1 Read each sentence in the chart. Decide if it uses a factual example or descriptive adjectives to support a general statement. Check (✓) the box in the correct column.

	FACTUAL EXAMPLE	DESCRIPTIVE ADJECTIVES
1. Arrive early for your interview. According to Working Women Weekly, you should arrive at least 10 minutes ahead of time.		
2. Good employers have many positive traits. For example, they are usually patient, flexible, and organized.		
3. Anyone can be a good networker. Studies show that shy people are equally good at networking as outgoing people.		
4. It is important to look for jobs by networking. Experts say only 20 percent of job openings are posted online or in newspapers.		
5. You may have to move for a new job. According to *Career* magazine, many companies require new employees to move.		
6. It is important to have a good attitude while you are job hunting. Be optimistic and patient during your search.		
7. A good cover letter is important. Your cover letter should be clear, organized, and specific.		
8. Career fairs are good places to network. According to experts, you will likely make at least three contacts at a career fair.		
9. Good job candidates have positive qualities. They are often polite, cheerful, and professional.		
10. Ask questions during your interview. Experts say you should ask at least six questions.		

2 Read these interview tips. Underline the phrases that introduce factual examples.

Top job interview tips

1 Dress for success! Experts say it may help to wear a suit.

2 Studies show that employers are twice as likely to remember candidates who smile. Remember to be friendly and polite.

3 Ask appropriate questions. Experts say you should be prepared to ask at least six questions.

4 According to *Industry* magazine, attentive listening is extremely important. Be sure to listen carefully and nod to show you understand.

5 Studies show that employers remember candidates who follow up quickly. Remember to write a thank-you note after your interview.

D. Skill Quiz

Check (✓) the correct answer for each item.

1 One reason to use specific examples in your writing is to

- a. make paragraphs longer.
- b. explain the meaning of adjectives.
- c. make writing more interesting.

2 Descriptive adjectives can make your writing more

- a. specific.
- b. general.
- c. boring.

3 A common phrase to show a factual example is

- a. *Research shows . . .*
- b. *Remember to . . .*
- c. *It is possible to . . .*

4 Choose the factual example from a paragraph about thank-you notes.

- a. Your thank-you note should be prompt, thoughtful, and friendly.
- b. Experts say that 80 percent of employers expect to receive thank-you notes.
- c. Remember to write a thank-you note.

5 Choose the example with descriptive adjectives from a paragraph about large companies.

- a. My ideal job is with a large, secure, and well-respected company.
- b. Large companies have 500 or more employees.
- c. Studies show that people who work at companies with fewer than 500 employees are often happy.

6 Choose the factual example from a paragraph about career fairs.

- a. My ideal job is with a large, secure, and well-respected company.
- b. Large companies have 500 or more employees.
- c. Studies show that people who work at companies with fewer than 500 employees are often happy.

7 Choose the example with descriptive adjectives that best supports this general statement: *Good employers share a number of positive traits.*

- a. They should write a thoughtful and polite thank-you note to the interviewer.
- b. They should write a clear and thorough résumé.
- c. They are usually patient and flexible.

8 Choose the factual example that supports this sentence: *Prepare for possible interview questions.*

- a. Research has shown that one of the most common interview topics is a successful project that the candidate has worked on.
- b. Studies show that people who smile often are more likely to get job offers.
- c. Research shows that it's important to follow up after an interview.

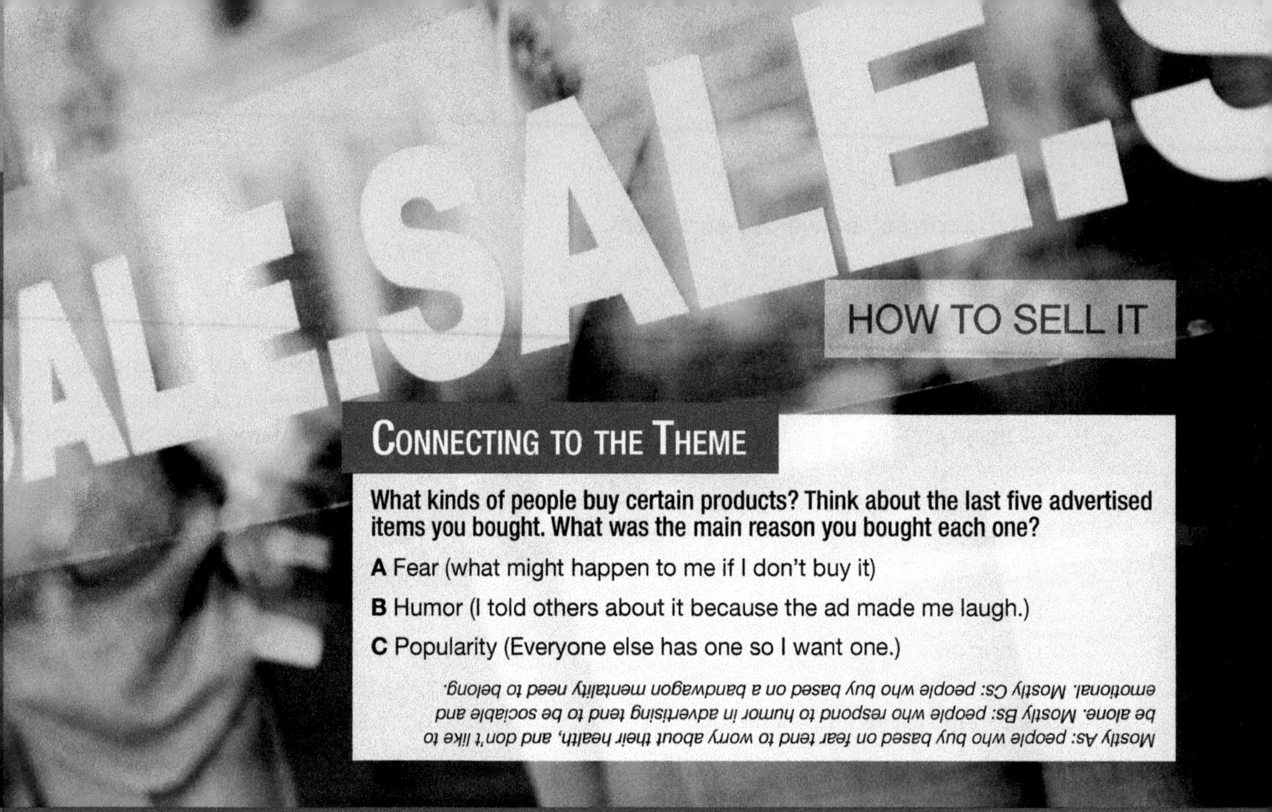

HOW TO SELL IT

Connecting to the Theme

What kinds of people buy certain products? Think about the last five advertised items you bought. What was the main reason you bought each one?

A Fear (what might happen to me if I don't buy it)

B Humor (I told others about it because the ad made me laugh.)

C Popularity (Everyone else has one so I want one.)

Mostly As: people who buy based on fear tend to worry about their health, and don't like to be alone. Mostly Bs: people who respond to humor in advertising tend to be sociable and emotional. Mostly Cs: people who buy based on a bandwagon mentality need to belong.

A. Skill Presentation

An **outline** summarizes, or briefly lists, the most important information in a piece of writing. Outlines help organize ideas from general to specific, or from big ideas down to the smallest ideas. Outlines have special formatting – they use letters and numbers, as well as indentation, to help organize ideas. Look at this outline for a paragraph about fear and humor in advertising.

MI Fear and humor in advertising often get consumers' attention.

1. Fear convinces people to buy.
    a. makes people feel unsafe
    b. people want a product to feel safe
2. Humor convinces people to buy.
    a. entertains people
    b. makes people laugh
    c. people feel good

MI Both of these advertising strategies can work well.

The outline starts with the **main idea** of the paragraph. The topic sentence usually states the main idea. At the end of the outline, the main idea is restated. This will be the concluding sentence of the paragraph.

The **supporting details** of the paragraph are listed underneath the main idea. You can use words or short phrases to summarize these details. The numbering (1 and 2) shows that these are the first and second supporting details. Notice that they are indented.

List specific **examples** underneath each supporting detail. You can use words or short phrases in an outline. The lowercase letters (a, b, and c) show that these are examples for each supporting detail. Notice that they are indented underneath the supporting details.

B. Over to You

1 Complete the outline with two correct supporting sentences.

They are creative. **Emotions affect what they buy.**
They spend a lot of money. **They understand advertising.**

People who make interesting ads have many abilities.

1 ____

a. want to explore new ideas
b. are often artistic

2 ____

a. know about consumers
b. can sell products

These abilities are important for making interesting ads.

2 Read the sentences from a paragraph, and decide if each sentence is the main idea, a supporting detail or reason, or an example. Check (✓) the box in the correct column.

	MAIN IDEA	SUPPORTING DETAIL OR REASON	EXAMPLE
1. Companies have different strategies to sell products.			
2. Some advertisers use fear to help them sell.			
3. One ad for a security alarm was scary to many people.			
4. The ad showed a thief entering a home.			
5. Some people got scared and decided to buy the alarm.			
6. On the other hand, some advertisers use humorous ads.			
7. For example, one funny commercial for a video store showed a dancing baby.			
8. This scene made many people laugh.			
9. They were entertained and wanted to buy videos.			
10. It is clear that different strategies can help companies sell different products.			

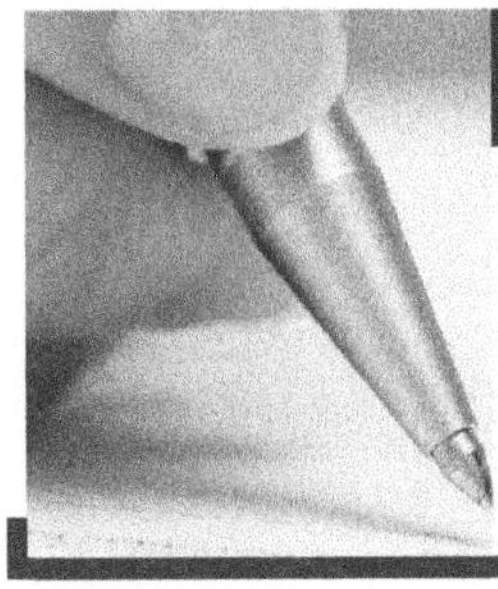

CHECK!

1 An outline helps __________ ideas and has special formatting.

2 One format for an outline lists the __________ idea (or topic sentence) at the beginning, and the concluding sentence at the end with __________ details or reasons listed next to numbers and __________ for each one listed next to letters.

C. Practice

1 Match each reason (1–5) with the correct example (a–e).

___ **1** Humorous ads can help sell products.

___ **2** Advertising is often quite expensive.

___ **3** Fear is an advertising strategy that works for some sellers.

___ **4** Advertisers hire creative people to make ads.

___ **5** Advertising often works when people pay attention.

a They have original ideas and can develop new approaches.
b One company spent $300,000 for a single television ad.
c It is easier to sell a product to someone who is watching and listening.
d One ad for car alarms shows a thief being chased by policemen.
e A shoe company used a popular comedian in its ads.

2 Look at the outlines, then number the sentences in the correct order.

1 Some advertisers use fear to sell products.
1. Selling smoke alarms
   a. house fire
   b. people worried
   c. emotion persuaded

Fear often convinces people to buy.

Some advertisers use fear to sell products.

___ This fearful emotion persuaded people to buy the alarm.

___ The advertisement made people worry about their family's safety.

___ One company was selling smoke alarms.

___ Fear often convinces people to buy.

___ Their ad showed a house fire.

2 Successful ads are sometimes entertaining.
1. Funny ads popular with young people
   a. pizza ad with comedian
   b. teenagers laughed

It is clear that entertaining ads can be very effective.

Successful ads are sometimes entertaining.

___ They thought eating pizza would make them feel good, too.

___ Teenagers who saw the ad laughed.

___ It is clear that entertaining ads can be very effective.

___ Some funny advertisements are popular with young people.

___ A pizza restaurant hired a comedian to tell jokes in its ads.

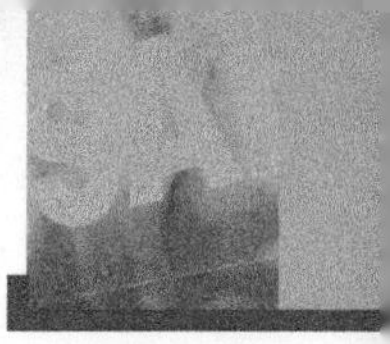

D. Skill Quiz

Check (✓) the correct answer for each item.

1 Outlines help
- ☐ a. organize ideas.
- ☐ b. change ideas.
- ☐ c. indent ideas.

2 Information in an outline is often
- ☐ a. expanded.
- ☐ b. plagiarized.
- ☐ c. summarized.

3 Where is the main idea found in an outline of a paragraph?
- ☐ a. next to every number
- ☐ b. underneath the supporting details
- ☐ c. at the beginning and the end

4 In an outline of a paragraph, supporting details (or reasons) and examples are always
- ☐ a. complete sentences.
- ☐ b. indented.
- ☐ c. persuasive.

5 Which of these sentences expresses the most general idea?
- ☐ a. Companies need to appeal to consumers so they buy their products.
- ☐ b. Advertising is not an easy business.
- ☐ c. Consumers see or hear 3,000 advertising messages every day.

6 Which of these sentences expresses the most specific idea?
- ☐ a. It is illegal for advertisements to give false information.
- ☐ b. There are many rules that advertisers must follow.
- ☐ c. Now advertising is everywhere.

7 When should you create an outline?
- ☐ a. After you have finished writing.
- ☐ b. In the middle of the writing process.
- ☐ c. Before you begin writing.

8 *There are many rules for advertising.*
   1. Strict for children's ads
      a. cannot be confusing

What is the main idea in the excerpt from this outline?
- ☐ a. There are many rules for advertising.
- ☐ b. Strict for children's ads
- ☐ c. cannot be confusing

9 *Advertisers often appeal to emotions.*
   1. Fear is used
      a. consumers may buy when afraid

What is the supporting detail in the excerpt from this outline?
- ☐ a. Advertisers often appeal to emotion.
- ☐ b. Fear is used
- ☐ c. consumers may buy when afraid

10 *Some humorous ads convince people to buy a product.*
   1. People remember funny, unusual things
      a. Dancing baby ad

What is the example in the excerpt from this outline?
- ☐ a. Some funny ads convince people to buy a product.
- ☐ b. Dancing baby ad
- ☐ c. humor made people want to buy

23

Review: Simple, Compound, and Complex Sentences

LIFE TODAY, LIFE TOMORROW

Connecting to the Theme

Are you happy where you are? How much do you agree with these statements?

A Strongly agree **B** Agree **C** Don't agree **D** Strongly disagree

I live in a clean environment with enough green space, like parks, to walk in.

I can ask my teachers questions when I need help, and my classes are not too crowded.

I can afford to live near college / my job.

I am confident I will be able to find a job after I leave college.

Mostly As and Bs: you are lucky – you are happy with where you live and study.

Mostly Cs and Ds: it sounds as if things could be better where you live.

A. Skill Presentation

Remember that using different types of sentences in your writing can add variety and interest.

A **simple sentence** has one independent clause. It has a subject and a verb, and it expresses one idea briefly and clearly.

ONE INDEPENDENT CLAUSE

The world population has increased slowly over time.

A **compound sentence** has more than one independent clause connected with a conjunction like *and, but, or,* or *so*. Compound sentences can express important relationships between two ideas. When you write, only combine sentences that are closely related to each other, and remember to add a comma before the conjunction.

INDEPENDENT CLAUSE — INDEPENDENT CLAUSE

Birth rates are declining in some countries, but they are increasing worldwide.

A **complex** sentence is a dependent clause that is combined with an independent clause to express a complete idea. A dependent clause often starts with a subordinating conjunction. *After, because, if* and *when* are examples of subordinating conjunctions.

INDEPENDENT CLAUSE — DEPENDENT CLAUSE

Death rates are decreasing because people are living longer.

Many dependent clauses can come before or after the independent clause. Remember to use a comma if the dependent clause comes first.

People started living longer after technology improved.

After technology improved, people started living longer.

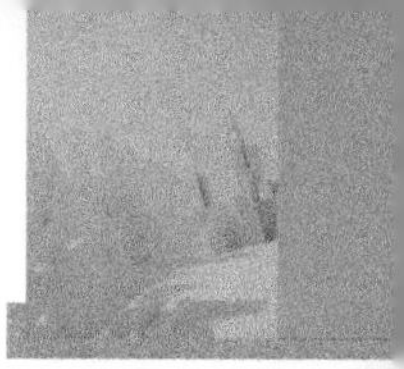

B. Over to You

1 Check (✓) the sentence that is more closely related to the sentence *There are more than 6.8 billion people in the world today.* Then combine the sentences using a conjunction.

1 ☐ There might be 2.2 billion more people by 2050.

2 ☐ There is another factor that affects the population explosion.

There are over 6.8 billion people in the world today ____

____.

2 Circle the correct subordinating conjunctions.

1 People started living longer *which* | *after* technology improved.

2 The environment may be in danger *if* | *although* the population explosion continues.

3 Read each sentence and decide what kind of sentence it is. Write *SS* for Simple Sentence, *CS* for Compound Sentence, or *CX* for Complex Sentence.

___ 1 Birth rates have been high recently, but death rates have been low.

___ 2 The number of humans in the world increased slowly.

___ 3 People are living longer than they did in the past.

___ 4 A larger world population may harm the environment, although no one is certain of this.

___ 5 After the plague ended in the 1400s, the world population increased.

___ 6 Many people have better healthcare now, so they live even longer.

___ 7 Birthrates are different from one country to another.

___ 8 Because many babies were born in the 1960s, the world population increased.

___ 9 Healthcare is an important topic these days.

___ 10 Healthy food recipes are common now, and many restaurants include nutrition information on their menu.

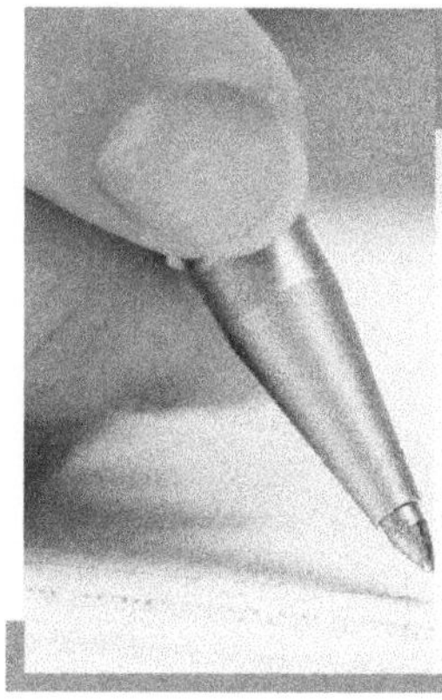

CHECK!

1 A __________ sentence has one independent clause.

2 A __________ sentence has more than one independent clause combined with a conjunction. Use a conjunction like *and*, *but*, *or*, or *so*. Remember to use a comma before the conjunction.

3 A __________ sentence has one independent clause combined with a dependent clause. A dependent clause often starts with a subordinating conjunction like *after*, *because*, *if*, or *when*. If the dependent clause comes first, follow it with a comma.

C. Practice

1 Read each sentence in the chart, and decide if it is a simple sentence, a compound sentence, or a complex sentence. Check (✓) the box in the correct column.

	SIMPLE	COMPOUND	COMPLEX
1. People are living longer than in the past.			
2. Life expectancy is the average number of years a person lives.			
3. The life expectancy of a person in the United States in the 1970s was 68 years, and in 2010 it was 76 years.			
4. Although they are not sure, experts think that by 2020 many people will live to be 78 years old.			
5. Life expectancy has increased 2.5 years each decade.			
6. Life expectancy will be 100 years by 2100 if this rate continues.			
7. If you were born after the year 2000, you are more likely to live to be 100.			
8. It may be good to live longer, but there may be some negative effects.			
9. An older population can cause economic problems in some countries.			
10. It is expensive to stay healthy for 100 years, and older people often require special care.			

2 Match each phrase (1–6) with the correct phrase (a–f) to make complete sentences.

1 You might think life was better 100 years ago, __

2 People had more children in the past, __

3 Today, even older people use technology, __

4 In general, people live longer today __

5 There are more people in the world today, __

6 Birth rates are declining, __

a because of recent medical advances.

b but they are not slowing down enough to stop the population explosion.

c so humans have a greater impact on the environment.

d or you might think it is better today.

e and it can help them stay connected to friends and relatives.

f but children often did not live as long.

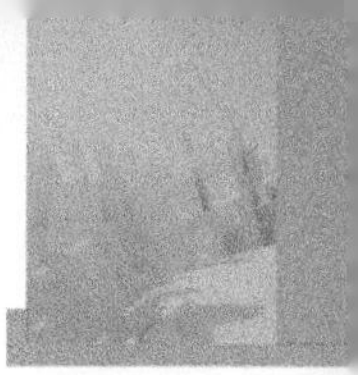

D. Skill Quiz

Check (✓) the correct answer for each item.

1 What is a simple sentence?

☐ a. a sentence with one independent clause
☐ b. a sentence with more than one independent clause
☐ c. a sentence with a dependent clause and at least one independent clause

2 What is a compound sentence?

☐ a. a sentence with one independent clause
☐ b. a sentence with more than one independent clause
☐ c. a sentence with a dependent clause and at least one independent clause

3 What is a complex sentence?

☐ a. a sentence with one independent clause
☐ b. a sentence with more than one independent clause
☐ c. a sentence with a dependent clause and at least one independent clause

4 Which conjunctions are used in compound sentences?

☐ a. *if*, *after*, and *since*
☐ b. *or*, *so*, and *but*
☐ c. *before*, *because*, and *although*

5 Which conjunctions are used in complex sentences?

☐ a. *and*, *nor*, and *for*
☐ b. *or*, *so*, and *but*
☐ c. *before*, *because*, and *although*

6 Choose the simple sentence.

☐ a. Life expectancy in 1900 was about 47 years in the United States.
☐ b. Life expectancy was lower in 1900 because life was difficult.
☐ c. Many people died at a young age, so life expectancy was low.

7 Choose the compound sentence.

☐ a. Birthrates are increasing, and death rates are declining.
☐ b. When birthrates and death rates are the same, the population is stable.
☐ c. Birthrates are declining in many countries around the world.

8 Choose the complex sentence.

☐ a. There was a population explosion in the United States in the 1960s.
☐ b. When many children were born during the "Baby Boom" of the 1950s, the population started to increase rapidly.
☐ c. Many children were born in the 1950s and 1960s, and they are called Baby Boomers.

9 Choose the sentence that shows correct comma use. If both sentences use the comma correctly, choose c.

☐ a. Although the population is increasing, many people are having smaller families.
☐ b. People in some countries, are having fewer children than people in other countries.
☐ c. Both a and b

10 Choose the sentence that shows correct comma use. If both sentences use the comma correctly, choose c.

☐ a. The population is increasing, and the environment may be at risk.
☐ b. Because the population is increasing, the environment may be at risk.
☐ c. Both a and b

24

Facts vs. Opinions

GETTING ALONG AT WORK

Connecting to the Theme

What do you think is acceptable behavior at work?

Yes No A co-worker keeps answering your phone pretending to be you.

Yes No A group of co-workers spend a lot of time smoking outside the office.

Yes No A co-worker spends most of his time telling jokes while everyone else is really busy.

Yes No A co-worker brings in cakes every day, and you are on a diet, but you can't resist.

In a survey of employees, the majority found all these behaviors unacceptable at work.

A. Skill Presentation

A **fact** is something that is true and can be proven. An **opinion** is a belief that cannot be proven. Others may disagree with an opinion. In academic writing, it is important to include facts to support opinions.

FACT: Thirteen employees work at the company.
(This is a fact. It can be proven by counting the number of employees at the company.)

OPINION: All the employees at that company are nice.
(This is an opinion. It cannot be proven. Other people may disagree that all the employees are nice.)

OPINION: Humor in the workplace offends everyone.
(This is an opinion. It is impossible to prove that everyone is offended by humor at work.)

FACT: My boss is Mr. Williams.
(This is a fact. It can be proven, and you can provide evidence for it.)

B. Over to You

1 Read the sentences and write *FACT* or *OPINION*.

__________ **1** Talia has worked here for ten months.

__________ **2** This is a great company.

__________ **3** The joke Dave told was very funny.

__________ **4** I had two other jobs before this one.

__________ **5** We finish work at 5:30 pm.

__________ **6** My boss is a very fair man.

__________ **7** More than 100 employees attended the office party.

__________ **8** The company is on two floors.

__________ **9** My boss moved here from Texas.

__________ **10** The office party was a lot of fun.

__________ **11** The office building needs to be redecorated.

__________ **12** The office building was built in 1920.

2 Read the paragraph and decide if each sentence is a fact or an opinion.

[1]Seri Sanders works for a bank. [2]She is a very hard worker. [3]She is good at her job. [4]Last week, one of her co-workers told a joke. [5]The employee who told the joke was rude. [6]Seri said she was offended and left the room. [7]The employee apologized to Seri at 4:30 that afternoon. [8]His apology was not sincere. [9]Now, Seri seems upset about the problem. [10]She made an appointment with her boss to ask for his advice.

The facts are sentences: __________ .

The opinions are sentences: __________ .

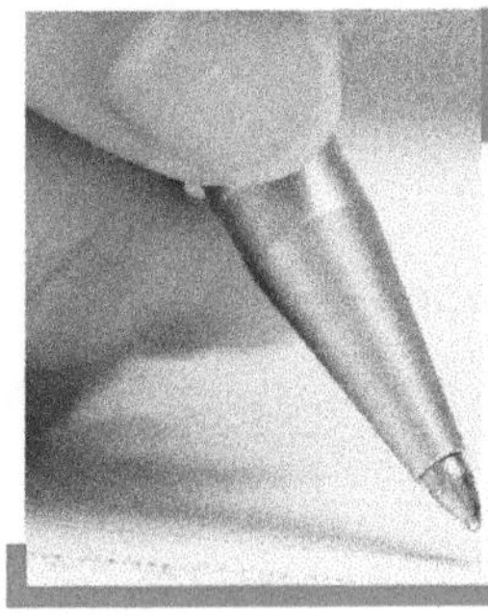

CHECK!

You should always use facts in your writing to support your opinions.

1 __________ :	2 __________ :
• true	• belief
• no one would disagree	• others may disagree
• can be proven	• cannot be proven

C. Practice

1 Read each sentence in the chart, and decide whether it is a fact or an opinion. Check (✓) the box in the correct column.

	FACT	OPINION
1. Bertha met with her boss last week.		
2. She told a joke.		
3. Everybody thought she was going to get in trouble.		
4. She told us a joke about engineers again yesterday.		
5. It was offensive.		
6. I think the boss took too long to deal with the situation.		
7. She told Bertha to apologize at the next meeting.		
8. Her behavior was extremely inappropriate.		
9. Three people sent written complaints last week.		
10. I asked her to stop telling jokes.		

2 Circle the correct facts to complete each sentence.

1 Tom and Sue had *a ten-minute* | *a helpful* | *an outrageous* argument in front of their co-workers.

2 Tom had to apologize *carefully* | *too many times* | *twice* before Sue would speak to him again.

3 Their argument happened *at 1:00 p.m.* | *at a bad time* | *in an inappropriate place.*

4 Sue is *hard to get along with,* | *Tom's boss* | *a difficult woman*, so Tom is worried about his job situation.

5 Three other employees *seemed annoyed* | *looked worried* | *heard the argument* and advised Tom to talk to Sue after work.

6 He worked *cheerfully* | *hard* | *overtime* to try to make Sue happy.

7 Sue started making outrageous demands and gave Tom *five more assignments* | *very difficult work* | *really boring tasks.*

8 Sue *thought he was rude* | *read Tom's apology note* | *felt offended.*

9 *Too many* | *Eight* | *Rude* employees listened to what happened in the meeting.

10 Soon, they heard laughter and *two* | *happy* | *humorous* voices. After the meeting, the workplace situation improved for everyone.

D. Skill Quiz

Check (✓) the correct answer for each item.

1 A fact

☐ a. can be invented.
☐ b. is impossible.
☐ c. can be proven.

2 An opinion is something that

☐ a. is always true.
☐ b. others may disagree with.
☐ c. can be counted.

3 In academic writing, you should

☐ a. use opinions to prove ideas.
☐ b. use facts to support opinions.
☐ c. use only opinions, never facts.

4 Which sentence is a fact?

☐ a. Travis and Hans are co-workers.
☐ b. Travis and Hans work well together.
☐ c. Travis and Hans are busy.

5 Which sentence is a fact?

☐ a. They are both humorous.
☐ b. They are both hard workers.
☐ c. They both work at CopleyTech.

6 Which sentence is an opinion?

☐ a. Hans and Travis have fun working together.
☐ b. Hans and Travis work together every weekend.
☐ c. Hans and Travis have never worked together.

7 Which sentence is a fact?

☐ a. Hans started working 50 hours a week.
☐ b. Hans was not working very hard.
☐ c. Hans was working too hard.

8 Which sentence is a fact?

☐ a. Travis is a kind and thoughtful person.
☐ b. Travis asked Hans what was wrong.
☐ c. Travis was very worried.

9 Which sentence is an opinion?

☐ a. Hans has worked there for a long time.
☐ b. Hans has worked there since last summer.
☐ c. Hans has worked there five years longer than Travis.

10 Which sentence is an opinion?

☐ a. Travis is an engineer.
☐ b. Travis is smart.
☐ c. Travis has a graduate degree.

25

Including Opposing Opinions

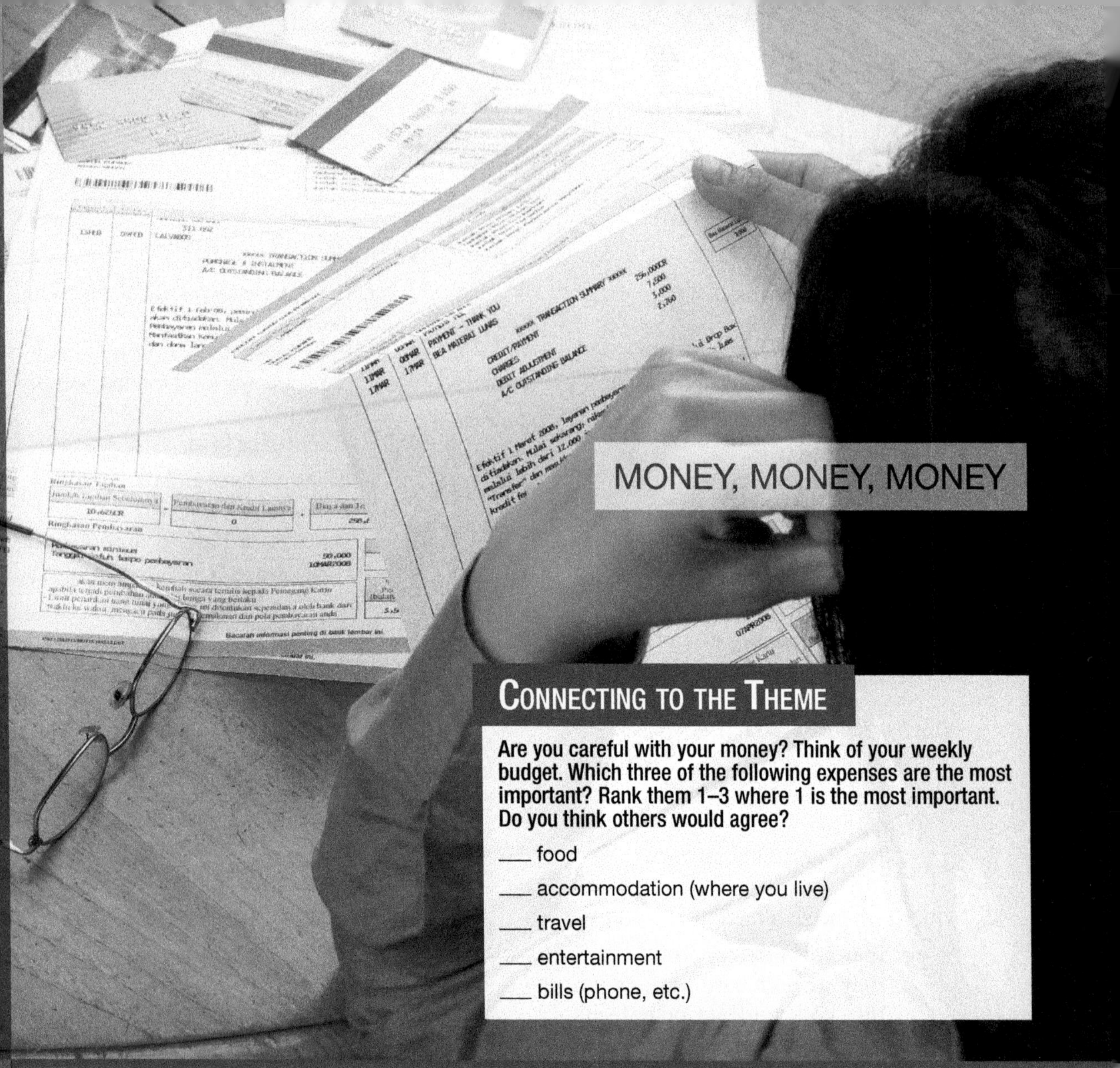

MONEY, MONEY, MONEY

Connecting to the Theme

Are you careful with your money? Think of your weekly budget. Which three of the following expenses are the most important? Rank them 1–3 where 1 is the most important. Do you think others would agree?

___ food

___ accommodation (where you live)

___ travel

___ entertainment

___ bills (phone, etc.)

A. Skill Presentation

When you make an argument in your writing, you first need to state your **opinion**. Your opinion is your belief about the main idea.

After stating your opinion, introduce an opinion that opposes yours. This is called a **counterargument**.

When you make an argument in your writing, it is also important to include a **refutation**. A **refutation** is a response to the counterargument. It brings readers back to your opinion and strengthens your opinion.

[O]People should avoid getting into debt.

[C]However, debts like student loans are necessary.

[R]To avoid unnecessary debt, find loans with low interest rates.

The refutation in this example responds to the counterargument by acknowledging that some loans may be necessary. It strengthens the opinion by arguing that too much debt should be avoided.

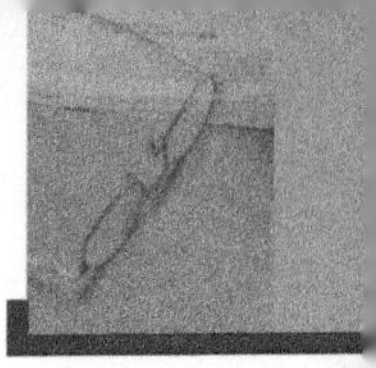

B. Over to You

1 Read the paragraphs and write *OPINION, COUNTERARGUMENT* or *REFUTATION* for each sentence.

1 [1]You should put as much money as possible in savings. [2]On the other hand, it is important to pay off credit card debt before saving money. [3]Try to save some money and pay off your credit cards each month.

1 ______________ 2 ______________ 3 ______________

2 [1]Students should be careful not to get into too much debt. [2]However, they have to pay for their studies and living costs while at school. [3]They should try to find part-time work to help with their costs while studying.

1 ______________ 2 ______________ 3 ______________

2 Match each initial opinion (1–8) with the correct counterargument (a–h).

___ **1** Using credit cards is easier than using cash.

___ **2** It is best to divide the cost of group dinners evenly.

___ **3** Owning a house is better than renting an apartment.

___ **4** It is important to take vacations to rest and relax.

___ **5** Buying a car is too expensive, so people should take public transportation instead.

___ **6** If you are on a budget, you should shop at inexpensive clothing stores.

___ **7** People should not take out loans.

___ **8** Staying home on weekends is a good way to save money.

a However, cheaper clothes may wear out more quickly than expensive ones.

b On the other hand, property taxes and home maintenance can cost more.

c However, you should not spend money on a trip if you are in debt.

d On the other hand, buses and trains are often expensive, too.

e However, you should not use credit cards too often.

f On the other hand, it is often necessary to borrow money for school.

g However, this may be unfair to people who choose cheaper meals.

h On the other hand, you could simply spend less on outside entertainment.

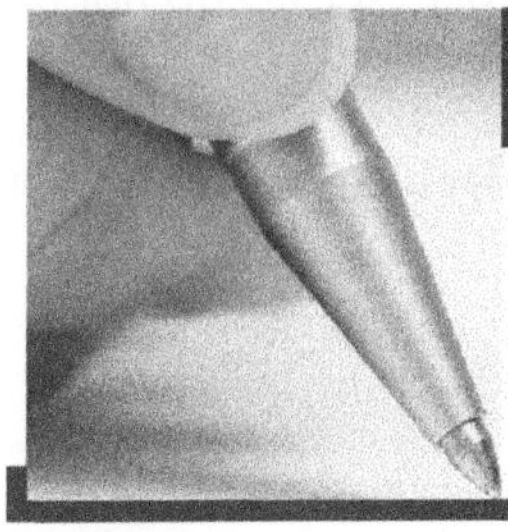

CHECK!

1 When you make an argument in your writing, state your ______________ and follow it with a ______________ that is different from your initial opinion.

2 Add a ______________ to respond to the counterargument and make your opinion stronger.

C. Practice

1 Read each opinion and check (✓) the correct counterargument.

1 The utility company should raise its prices.

- ☐ a. Some people think the utility company's prices should increase.
- ☐ b. Some people think the utility company should spend less money instead of raising prices.
- ☐ c. Some people think the utility company provides a good service.

2 Parents should give their children a weekly allowance.

- ☐ a. However, children should not get an allowance unless they earn it.
- ☐ b. However, children should get at least $10 for allowance.
- ☐ c. However, children should try to do well in school.

3 The government should spend more money on scientific research.

- ☐ a. On the other hand, it is more important to spend money on education.
- ☐ b. On the other hand, scientific research should be a priority.
- ☐ c. On the other hand, many scientists make important contributions.

4 People should not take out loans.

- ☐ a. However, it is important to avoid borrowing money.
- ☐ b. However, debt can be difficult to pay off.
- ☐ c. However, home and school loans are often necessary.

5 The government should raise taxes to build new roads.

- ☐ a. On the other hand, private companies could spend more money on roads.
- ☐ b. A tax increase would help pay for new roads.
- ☐ c. We need new roads all around the country, not just in our state.

2 Number the sentences in order. Put the opinion first, the counterargument second, and the refutation third.

1 ___ On the other hand, you should have a fund for unexpected expenses at any age.
___ Therefore, you should save at least 15 percent of your income regardless of your age.
___ Saving money is less urgent when you are young.

2 ___ However, cutting a small expense, such as a cup of coffee, can be easier.
___ Cutting both large and small expenses may be the best way to save money.
___ When saving money, it is most effective to cut large expenses.

3 ___ However, teenagers may need a cell phone to learn about new job openings and apply for them.
___ Teenagers should have a small, inexpensive cell phone plan if they do not have a job.
___ Teenagers should not have a cell phone if they do not have a job.

4 ___ Electronics stores have sales, so even a person on a budget can sometimes buy new electronic devices.
___ However, new electronic devices are often expensive.
___ It's best to buy new electronic devices.

D. Skill Quiz

Check (✓) the correct answer for each item.

1 An opinion that seems to oppose yours is called

- ☐ a. a counterargument.
- ☐ b. a refutation.
- ☐ c. an initial opinion.

2 A refutation

- ☐ a. strengthens your counterargument.
- ☐ b. strengthens your opinion.
- ☐ c. strengthens your opponent.

3 Adding a counterargument and refutation

- ☐ a. strengthens your argument.
- ☐ b. weakens your argument.
- ☐ c. makes your argument too complicated.

4 Choose the opinion.

- ☐ a. However, some people think children should only get money for doing chores.
- ☐ b. Therefore, parents should give children an allowance after they do their chores each week.
- ☐ c. Parents should give their children a weekly allowance.

5 Choose the counterargument.

- ☐ a. However, some people think children should only get money for doing chores.
- ☐ b. Therefore, parents should give children an allowance after they do their chores each week.
- ☐ c. Parents should give their children a weekly allowance.

6 Choose the refutation.

- ☐ a. However, some people think children should only get money for doing chores.
- ☐ b. Therefore, parents should give children an allowance after they do their chores each week.
- ☐ c. Parents should give their children a weekly allowance.

7 Choose the counterargument to this initial opinion: *People on a budget should not buy expensive electronic equipment.*

- ☐ a. However, many people like to own electronic equipment.
- ☐ b. However, it is possible to buy electronic equipment on sale.
- ☐ c. However, people who are in debt should not buy electronic equipment.

8 Choose the counterargument to this opinion: *An easy way to save money is to bring your lunch to work.*

- ☐ a. Buying lunch at restaurants can cost almost $1,500 a year.
- ☐ b. The best way to save money is to not eat lunch.
- ☐ c. Some people do not have time to make their lunch every morning.

26

Transition Words 2: Examples and Contrasts

WE ARE ALL DIFFERENT

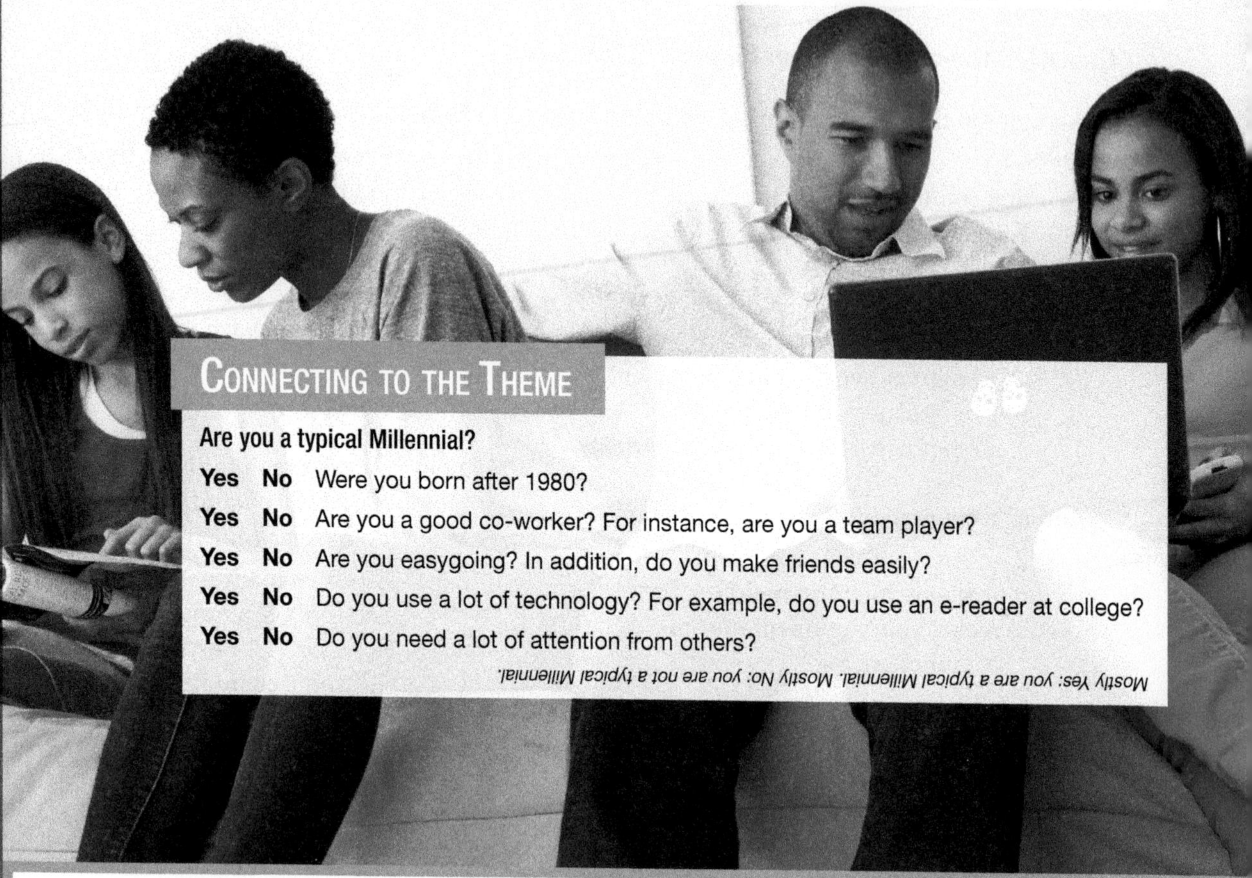

CONNECTING TO THE THEME

Are you a typical Millennial?

Yes No Were you born after 1980?

Yes No Are you a good co-worker? For instance, are you a team player?

Yes No Are you easygoing? In addition, do you make friends easily?

Yes No Do you use a lot of technology? For example, do you use an e-reader at college?

Yes No Do you need a lot of attention from others?

Mostly Yes: you are a typical Millennial. Mostly No: you are not a typical Millennial.

A. Skill Presentation

Remember that **transition words** are words that show connections between ideas. They are very important in writing. They help ideas in a paragraph make sense.

Some transition words are used to show examples. They give information to explain an idea in a previous sentence. Use the transition words *for example* and *for instance* to give examples.

> Millennials are Americans born between 1980 and the early twenty-first century. Millennials have certain things in common. **For example**, they usually work well in teams.

Other transition words are used to give more information about an idea or to build on it. Use the transition words *in addition*, *moreover*, and *furthermore* to give more information.

> **Furthermore**, many Millennials also know a lot about technology.

Some transition words are used to show contrast. They show that an idea is different from an idea in a previous sentence. Use the transition words *in contrast*, *on the other hand*, and *however* to show contrasting ideas.

> Some people say it is impossible to describe large groups of people based on when they were born. **However**, it is clear that our world affects us. That world is different from one time to another.

Transition words usually go at the beginning of a sentence. Remember to always put a comma after transition words.

B. Over to You

1 Read the sentences about Millennials, and circle the correct transition words.

1 Millennials are comfortable with technology. *For instance,* | *After that,* they are good at sending text messages.

2 Millennials can seem immature. *To start,* | *In addition,* they can seem spoiled.

3 Millennials balance work with their personal lives. *For example,* | *In contrast,* some older people put work before personal interests.

2 Read each sentence in the chart. Decide if it is giving an example, giving more information, or showing contrast. Check (✓) the box in the correct column.

	GIVING AN EXAMPLE	GIVING MORE INFORMATION	SHOWING CONTRAST
1. For example, young people can be spoiled.			
2. In addition, Millennials are often friendly.			
3. In contrast, older people are more easygoing.			
4. Moreover, she is conservative.			
5. For instance, my sister knows a lot about computers.			
6. On the other hand, my siblings are hard workers.			
7. Furthermore, they work well as a team.			
8. However, they can be adventurous.			
9. In contrast, older people are less adventurous.			
10. Furthermore, the teenagers from next door agreed to help plant the community garden.			

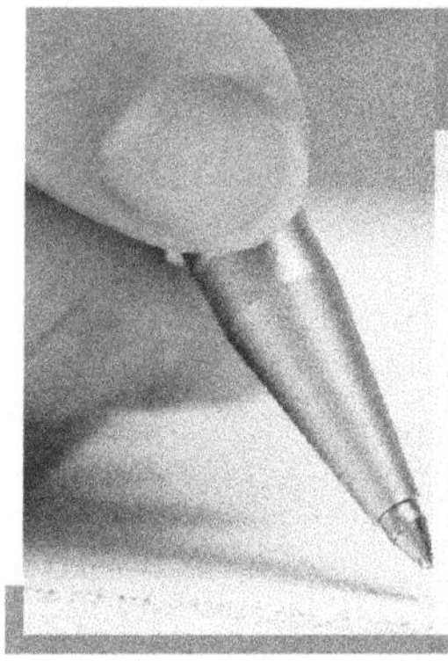

CHECK!

1 You can use the transition words *for instance* to give an __________.

2 You can use the transition words *moreover* and *furthermore* to give more __________ about an idea.

3 You can use the transition words *on the other hand* and *however* to show __________ ideas.

4 These transition words usually go at the __________ of a sentence. Remember to use a comma after them.

C. Practice

1 Read the paragraphs. How many transition words are there?

A [1]*Gen Xers* were born in the 1970s and the 1980s. [2]In these decades, both parents often worked. [3]This made many young Gen Xers independent. [4]For instance, some of them came home to an empty house. [5]When they did this, they sometimes had to make their own dinner.

[6]Gen Xers' parents are "Baby Boomers." [7]They often struggle with technology. [8]However, Gen Xers are usually good with technology. [9]Gen Xers are often flexible. [10]Furthermore, they like freedom and often reject rules. [11]Of course, these are general statements.

There are ___ transition words. Sentences: ___________

B [1]Some people believe that birth order has a big impact on your personality. [2]For example, younger children often experience more freedom than older children. [3]It is often the youngest child who is the most adventurous and daring. [4]In contrast, an older sibling (brother or sister) may be more conservative and take fewer risks. [5]For instance, a younger child may try dangerous activities, but an older sibling may not. [6]Moreover, parents tend not to discipline their younger children as much as their older ones. [7]Studies have shown that younger children are extremely independent. [8]On the other hand, research has shown that siblings who are close to each other live happier lives.

There are ___ transition words. Sentences: ___________

2 Match each sentences (1–5) with the correct transition word sentence (a–e).

___ **1** Many important events happened when Baby Boomers were young adults.

___ **2** Baby Boomers' children are usually good at learning new technology.

___ **3** Female Baby Boomers began to have more personal freedom in the 1970s.

___ **4** Baby Boomers often focus on individual choices.

___ **5** Today, many Baby Boomers are helping their children.

a For example, this generation was in their 20s during the Civil Rights Movement.

b Furthermore, they are taking care of their elderly parents.

c However, they like to make group decisions at work.

d In contrast, Baby Boomers often find it difficult to use new computers.

e Moreover, they had more opportunities in the workplace.

D. Skill Quiz

Check (✓) the correct answer for each item.

1 What do transition words do?

☐ a. They always come at the end of sentences.
☐ b. They only show contrasting ideas in writing.
☐ c. They connect ideas in writing.

2 What do transition words that give examples do?

☐ a. They introduce unnecessary information about an idea.
☐ b. They introduce specific information to explain an idea.
☐ c. They show an idea that is different.

3 What do transition words that introduce more information do?

☐ a. They build on an idea.
☐ b. They tell why an idea is wrong.
☐ c. They state a reason for the main idea.

4 What do transition words that show contrast do?

☐ a. They give additional information about an idea.
☐ b. They give specific information to illustrate an idea.
☐ c. They show an idea that is different.

5 Choose the sentence that gives an example of this idea: *Baby Boomers often had strict parents.*

☐ a. In addition, Baby Boomers often had conservative parents.
☐ b. For instance, Baby Boomers had to follow a lot of rules.
☐ c. However, Baby Boomers are usually responsible.

6 Choose the sentence that gives more information about this idea: *Millennials often care about the environment.*

☐ a. Furthermore, they are often upset about the pollution caused by cars and trucks.
☐ b. On the other hand, they may not be as concerned with civil rights
☐ c. For instance, they think it is important to recycle.

7 Choose the sentence that contrasts this idea: *Television was invented before Gen Xers were born.*

☐ a. For example, many Gen Xers still watch TV frequently.
☐ b. In contrast, some Baby Boomers were born before TVs were common.
☐ c. Moreover, they grew up watching TV.

8 Choose the sentence that uses a comma correctly.

☐ a. In addition you may, have a lot in common with people your age.
☐ b. In addition you may have a lot in common, with people your age.
☐ c. In addition, you may have a lot in common with people your age.

27

Formal vs. Informal Vocabulary and Using Vivid Language

THE BEST AND THE WORST

Connecting to the Theme

You have been asked to create two posters to promote two events to raise money for an earthquake disaster fund. Can you choose three appropriate informal phrases for a student campus event and three appropriate formal phrases for a city hall event?

- Your support needed!
- Hey guys!
- Get down to our fundraising event.
- Please come along to this fundraising event
- Every dollar counts. Please give generously.
- Any spare dime makes a difference.

Student Campus: Hey guys! Get down to our fundraising event. Any spare dime you've got makes a difference. City Hall: Your support needed! Please come along to this fundraising event. Every dollar counts. Please give generously.

A. Skill Presentation

Some ideas can be expressed with either formal or informal vocabulary.

MORE FORMAL	MORE INFORMAL
children	kids
dollar	buck
police	cops

It is important to remember that academic writing is usually formal. For example, a college essay uses more formal vocabulary and grammar than an e-mail to a friend. Personal e-mails and text messages are usually examples of informal writing.

It is also important to make your writing clear and interesting. One way to do this is to use **vivid language.** Vivid language helps your reader understand exactly what you are writing about and also makes your writing more interesting.

To make the language in your writing vivid, choose words that are as specific and descriptive as possible.

A big flood destroyed the city.

In this example, the word *big* could be more specific.

A major flood destroyed the city.

A word like *major* is more specific and helps make this sentence clearer and more interesting.

B. Over to You

1 Read the sentences and decide if the words in bold are more formal or more informal. Write *FORMAL* or *INFORMAL*.

__________ 1 Some **guys** were helping the earthquake victim.

__________ 2 Some **men** were helping the earthquake victim.

2 Read the sentences and decide if the words in bold are less vivid or more vivid. Write *LESS VIVID* or *MORE VIVID*.

__________ 1 The flood was **huge and serious**.

__________ 2 The flood was **big and bad**.

3 Match each formal word (1–10) with the correct more informal word (a–j).

___ **1** children	**a** mess up
___ **2** money	**b** hi
___ **3** strike (verb)	**c** cops
___ **4** man	**d** useful
___ **5** police	**e** happen
___ **6** develop (verb)	**f** kids
___ **7** people	**g** make
___ **8** effective	**h** cash
___ **9** damage (verb)	**i** guy
___ **10** hello	**j** folks

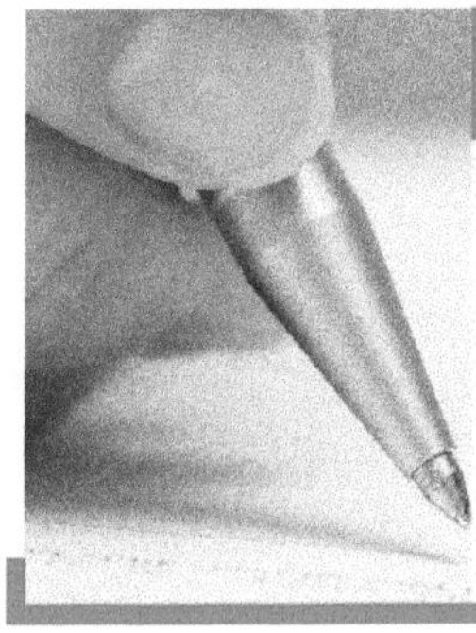

CHECK!

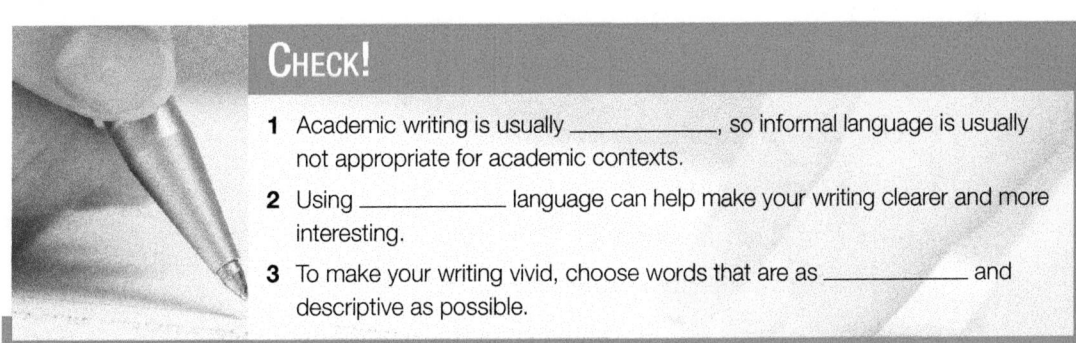

1 Academic writing is usually __________, so informal language is usually not appropriate for academic contexts.

2 Using __________ language can help make your writing clearer and more interesting.

3 To make your writing vivid, choose words that are as __________ and descriptive as possible.

C. Practice

1 Read the e-mails from students to their professors. Underline the sentences that have words that are too informal.

To: Professor Joyner
Subject: Earthquake discussion
From: Paulo

Professor Joyner,
[1]I enjoyed our discussion about earthquakes last week. [2]It is interesting that people besides cops and firefighters give relief. [3]I was surprised how many guys travel from far away to help victims. [4]I would like to dedicate some of my time to help. [5]Do you think we could raise money to pay for our own trip?
Have a good day,
Paulo

To: Professor Braun
Subject: Final project
From: Meagan

Dear Professor Braun,
[1]For my final project, I would like to write an essay about floods. [2]There is a lot of stuff to cover. [3]For example, a lot of folks lose their belongings. [4]Adults and kids are both affected. [5]Please let me know if this is a good idea for a project.
Thank you,
Meagan

2 Circle the more vivid words.

1 A tornado *hit* | *came* to the area ten years ago.
2 The earthquake was *powerful* | *big*.
3 I was *afraid* | *terrified* when I saw the tornado.
4 *Major* | *Big* disasters can happen anywhere.
5 *People* | *Residents* were not prepared for the hurricane.
6 Earthquakes can *happen* | *strike* without any warning.
7 Finding money to rebuild after a disaster can be *hard* | *challenging*.
8 The state *developed* | *made* a better plan for the future.
9 When there is a *serious* | *bad* disaster, people need to help each other.
10 Emergency vehicles *drove* | *rushed* to the scene.

D. Skill Quiz

Check (✓) the correct answer for each item.

1 An example of more formal writing is

- ☐ a. an e-mail to a professor.
- ☐ b. an e-mail to your study group members.
- ☐ c. a text message to a friend.

2 More formal English should be used for

- ☐ a. research papers.
- ☐ b. e-mails to your roommate.
- ☐ c. notes to friends.

3 Which is an example of informal, nonacademic writing?

- ☐ a. An essay for a history class
- ☐ b. A personal note to a classmate
- ☐ c. An application essay for a scholarship

4 Vivid language is usually

- ☐ a. more general.
- ☐ b. imprecise.
- ☐ c. more specific.

5 Choose the most informal word.

- ☐ a. information
- ☐ b. stuff
- ☐ c. objects

6 Choose the word to complete this sentence from a research paper: *The earthquake occurred suddenly and frightened the* ___

- ☐ a. residents.
- ☐ b. folks.
- ☐ c. guys.

7 Choose the more informal word in this sentence: *Some folks helped the children.*

- ☐ a. folks
- ☐ b. helped
- ☐ c. children

8 Which greeting is most formal in English?

- ☐ a. Hey!
- ☐ b. Hello!
- ☐ c. Hi!

9 Which word is an example of more informal English?

- ☐ a. guy
- ☐ b. man
- ☐ c. gentleman

10 The word *cops* is

- ☐ a. more formal.
- ☐ b. more informal.
- ☐ c. incorrect.

MANAGING YOUR BODY CLOCK

CONNECTING TO THE THEME

All living things are changing all day, every day. Scientists call this the *circadian rhythm*. How much do you know about circadian rhythms? Are these statements true or false?

1 Most adults sleep about eight hours a night.

2 The morning is the best time to exercise.

3 Most people's body temperature is lowest at 10 o'clock in the evening.

4 Most people's body temperature is highest at 7 o'clock in the evening.

5 Sleeping in a dark room helps prevent sleep cycle disturbances.

1 True, 2 False (the afternoon is the best time to exercise), 3 False (most people's body temperature is lowest at 10 o'clock in the morning), 4 True, 5 True.

A. Skill Presentation

It is important for most academic writing to have a formal tone. You can follow these guidelines to help make your writing sound more formal.

Use the third person instead of *I*, *me*, and *my*. Using the third person helps you to sound less personal and more objective. It is important to be less personal and more objective when you write because academic writing focuses on facts and well-supported opinions, not on personal experiences. Also, avoid using the second-person pronoun *you*. Be specific about who you are talking about.

I sleep better when I have exercised during the day. ✗

People who exercise during the day usually sleep better. ✓

In this sentence, *people* is more specific than *you*.

Avoid contractions. Contractions connect two words with an apostrophe. For example, *don't*, *there's*, and *isn't* are all contractions. In academic writing, use full forms instead. *Do not*, *there is*, and *is not* sound more academic.

It's not a good idea to drink coffee after 5 o'clock if you want a good night's sleep. ✗

It is not a good idea to drink coffee after 5 o'clock because it can make sleep difficult. ✓

B. Over to You

1 Read the sentences about healthy lifestyles. Decide if they are academic or non-academic in tone. Write *ACADEMIC* or *NON-ACADEMIC*.

________________ **1** I believe it's important to exercise at least four times a week. Lots of people enjoy running and lifting weights.

________________ **2** Scientists recommend that adults sleep for at least eight hours a night.

________________ **3** Scientists do not know if all plants have the same circadian rhythm. However, they are certain that plants operate on a 24-hour cycle.

2 Circle the correct words to give the text a more formal tone.

1 When *humans are* | *you're* sleeping, *you* | *they* go through four stages. The first stage is called "light sleep." When people are in light sleep, they can wake up easily

2 In the second stage, the brain slows down. *It's* | *It is* more difficult to wake *someone* | *you* up when you're in this stage.

3 In the third and fourth stages, R.E.M., or Rapid Eye Movement, occurs. R.E.M. usually happens when *a person is* | *you're* having detailed dreams. *You* | *Most people* probably experience R.E.M. at least three times each night.

4 If the third or fourth sleep cycle is interrupted, *it'll probably have* | *there may be* negative effects on the body. To prevent waking up during the night, *you* | *some people* can take precautions. Some doctors advise their patients to sleep in a dark bedroom.

5 *It is probably not a good idea to* | *You should not* sleep with music or the television on. Relaxing activities, such as reading or stretching, may also help *you* | *people* sleep better.

6 *People* | *You* who have trouble sleeping should probably try to take naps to avoid becoming overtired. *Those who nap* | *you* probably get more sleep that way.

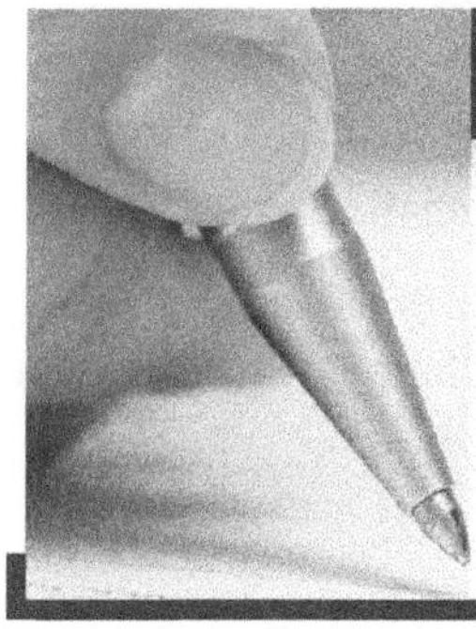

CHECK!

1 In academic writing, try to be less personal and more ____________. Be ____________ about who you are talking about.

2 Use the ____________ person instead of *I*, *me*, and *my*, and avoid using the ____________ -person pronoun *you*.

3 Contractions connect two words with an ____________. In academic writing, use ____________ forms instead.

C. Practice

1 Read each sentence in the chart, and decide if it has a more formal or informal tone. Check (✓) the box in the correct column.

	MORE FORMAL	MORE INFORMAL
1. It's important to get enough sleep.		
2. When I drink coffee at night, I have a hard time falling asleep.		
3. Scientists recommend that adults exercise at least three times a week.		
4. Studies have shown that most people sleep seven to eight hours each night.		
5. My muscles work best in the afternoon.		
6. Some doctors think that you shouldn't drink too much caffeine.		
7. To avoid disturbing the sleep cycle, doctors recommend that people sleep in dark bedrooms.		
8. Jet lag is considered a circadian rhythm sleep disorder.		
9. If you're a professional athlete, jet lag can hurt your performance.		
10. Melatonin is a chemical that affects the circadian rhythm.		

2 Read each group of sentences. Check (✓) the sentence with the most formal tone and objective-sounding language.

1 ☐ a. Some women discover they are pregnant when they start to have trouble sleeping.
☐ b. I knew I was pregnant because I started to have trouble sleeping.
☐ c. If you are pregnant, you might have trouble sleeping.

2 ☐ a. Jet lag might keep you from sleeping well for several days.
☐ b. Jet lag may prevent a traveler from sleeping normally for several days.
☐ c. Jet lag prevented me from getting a good night's sleep for several days.

3 ☐ a. Employees who often have to work late may suffer from sleep disorders.
☐ b. If your job requires you to work late, you might suffer from a sleep disorder.
☐ c. Whenever I have to work late, I have trouble sleeping.

4 ☐ a. Doctors say that short naps do not affect the sleep cycle.
☐ b. My doctor says that short naps won't affect my sleep cycle.
☐ c. Doctors say that short naps won't affect your sleep cycle.

5 ☐ a. There's evidence that some medicines can interrupt your sleep cycle.
☐ b. There is evidence that some medicines can interrupt the sleep cycle.
☐ c. If you take certain medicines, your sleep cycle might be interrupted.

6 ☐ a. In the winter, many people go to sleep earlier.
☐ b. In the winter, I go to sleep earlier.
☐ c. In the winter, you usually go to sleep earlier than in the summer.

D. Skill Quiz

Check (✓) the correct answer for each item.

1 Academic writing usually has

- ☐ a. a more formal tone.
- ☐ b. a more informal tone.
- ☐ c. a more personal tone.

2 In academic writing it is often important to include only facts and well-supported opinions. This is called being

- ☐ a. detailed.
- ☐ b. subjective.
- ☐ c. objective.

3 To achieve a more academic tone in your writing, avoid

- ☐ a. all pronouns.
- ☐ b. full forms.
- ☐ c. *I*, *me*, and *my*.

4 Contractions may give your writing

- ☐ a. a very formal tone.
- ☐ b. a less formal tone.
- ☐ c. a specific tone.

i To avoid jet lag, you can take a few simple precautions.
ii It's important to sleep on the plane. If it helps, you can bring sleep aids such as earplugs or a sleep mask.

5 In the sentences above, which change to i would make it more formal?

- ☐ a. To avoid jet lag, I take a few simple precautions.
- ☐ b. To avoid jet lag, travelers can take a few simple precautions.
- ☐ c. To avoid jet lag, you should take a few simple precautions.

6 In the sentences above **5**, which change to ii would make it more formal?

- ☐ a. It's important to sleep on the plane. If it helps, you can bring sleep aids such as earplugs or a sleep mask.
- ☐ b. It's important to sleep on the plane. If it helps you, bring sleep aids such as earplugs or a sleep mask.
- ☐ c. It is important to sleep on the plane. If it helps, travelers can bring sleep aids such as earplugs or a sleep mask.

i There's evidence that pregnant women often have trouble sleeping.
ii If you're having trouble sleeping, don't hesitate to talk to your doctor.

7 In the sentences above, which change to i would make it more formal?

- ☐ a. If you are pregnant, you may have trouble sleeping.
- ☐ b. When I was pregnant, I often had trouble sleeping.
- ☐ c. There is evidence that pregnant women often have trouble sleeping.

8 In the sentences above, which change to ii would make it more formal?

- ☐ a. If you're having trouble sleeping, you should talk to your doctor.
- ☐ b. People who are having trouble sleeping shouldn't hesitate to talk to their doctor.
- ☐ c. People who are having trouble sleeping should not hesitate to talk to their doctor.

29

Review: Combining Sentences

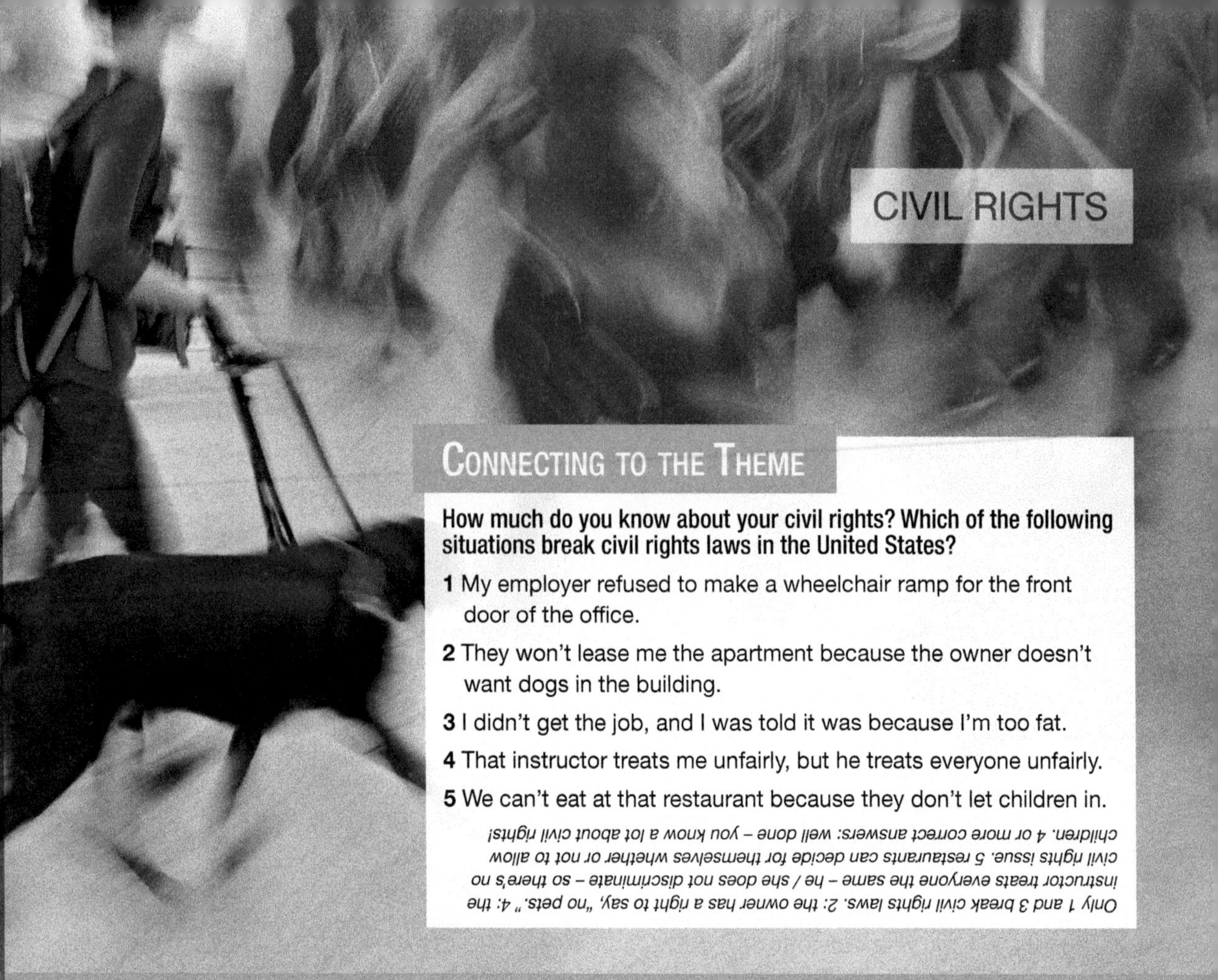

CIVIL RIGHTS

Connecting to the Theme

How much do you know about your civil rights? Which of the following situations break civil rights laws in the United States?

1 My employer refused to make a wheelchair ramp for the front door of the office.

2 They won't lease me the apartment because the owner doesn't want dogs in the building.

3 I didn't get the job, and I was told it was because I'm too fat.

4 That instructor treats me unfairly, but he treats everyone unfairly.

5 We can't eat at that restaurant because they don't let children in.

Only 1 and 3 break civil rights laws. 2: the owner has a right to say, "no pets." 4: the instructor treats everyone the same – he / she does not discriminate – so there's no civil rights issue. 5 restaurants can decide for themselves whether or not to allow children. 4 or more correct answers: well done – you know a lot about civil rights!

A. Skill Presentation

Remember that a complete sentence must have a subject and a verb. A sentence that is missing a subject or a verb – including an auxiliary verb – is one kind of **sentence fragment**. Sentence fragments are not grammatically correct. For example, this sentence doesn't have an auxiliary verb:

> They struggling for years. ✗
> They **were** struggling for years. ✓

Another kind of fragment is a dependent clause by itself. A dependent clause may have a subject and a verb, but it needs to be combined with an independent clause to make a complete sentence.

> Before the law changed. ✗
> They were struggling for years before the law changed. ✓

In a compound sentence, independent clauses must be joined by a comma and a conjunction. If there is no comma or no conjunction, it is a **run-on sentence**. Run-on sentences are not grammatically correct.

> A blind person wants to live in an apartment it does not allow pets. ✗
> A blind person wants to live in an apartment, **but** it does not allow pets. ✓

If only a comma joins independent clauses in a compound sentence, it is called a **comma splice**. Comma splices are not grammatically correct. Remember to include a conjunction.

> Everyone has a right to fair housing, people who discriminate are breaking the law. ✗
> Everyone has a right to fair housing, **and** people who discriminate are breaking the law. ✓

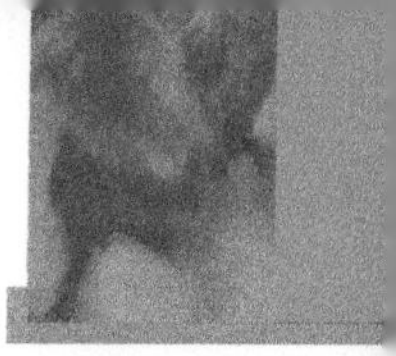

B. Over to You

1 Read the sentences and decide if they are correct or incorrect. Write *CORRECT* or *INCORRECT*.

__________ 1 If the person needs a service dog, too.

__________ 2 The building makes an exception if the person needs a service dog.

__________ 3 It is illegal to discriminate against the disabled, and it is also illegal to discriminate against the elderly.

__________ 4 It is illegal to discriminate against the disabled it is also illegal to discriminate against the elderly.

2 Read each item in the chart. Decide if it is a sentence fragment, a run-on sentence, a comma splice, or a correct sentence. Check (✓) the box in the correct column.

	SENTENCE FRAGMENT	RUN-ON SENTENCE	COMMA SPLICE	CORRECT
1. There were many heroes during the Civil Rights Movement.				
2. Mary McLeod Bethune created schools for African American students she encouraged them to get a good education.				
3. Ruby Bridges helped end segregation in schools.				
4. Jesse Jackson worked to get equal jobs for African Americans, he worked with Martin Luther King, Jr.				
5. Because he was president during the Civil Rights Movement.				
6. Rosa Parks sat in the "white" section of the bus, she was arrested.				
7. Homer Plessy fought against discrimination on trains he won the fight.				
8. Martin Luther King, Jr. fighting to get rights for African Americans.				

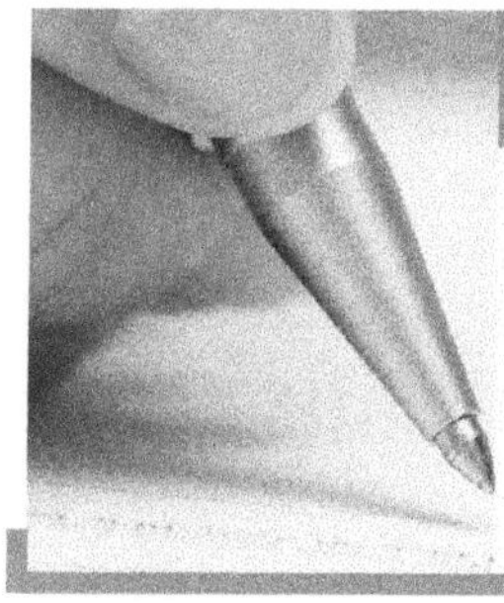

CHECK!

1 Sentences must have a __________ and a __________.

2 A dependent clause needs to be combined with an __________ clause to make a complete sentence.

3 In a compound sentence, independent clauses must be joined by a __________ and a comma.

C. Practice

1 Add a comma to correct each run-on sentence.

1 The Equal Employment Opportunity Act is a law in the United States and it was passed in 1972.

2 People cannot be discriminated against at work based on their race and they cannot be discriminated against for their age.

3 The act was changed in 1995 so now it protects other people, as well.

4 The new act protects the disabled and it also protects people with different political beliefs.

5 The act protects people at work but it does not protect people in their homes.

6 The Equal Pay Act (EPA) protects workers and it makes employers pay men and women equally.

7 Many women worked for less money than men in the 1940s so they fought for equality.

8 Employers have to pay women equally but some women still fight for their rights at work.

9 Many women working today are young and they do not have the same challenges women used to have.

10 Some people want to share their knowledge about the EPA so they have written books about its history.

11 Men and women should be paid equally for doing the same job and the job title shouldn't be an issue.

12 Many men stay at home with the children today and women earn the majority of the family's income.

2 Read the paragraph. How many comma splices are there?

[1]Ruby Bridges Nell was important in the Civil Rights Movement. [2]She was born in Mississippi in 1954, she moved to New Orleans when she was four. [3]Ruby lived a few blocks from a "white" school, she attended an African American school several miles away. [4]When Ruby was six, schools in New Orleans were no longer segregated. [5]However, African American students had to take a test to get into to the "white" schools. [6]Ruby passed the test, she was the first African American student to attend an all-white school. [7]She started school in October of 1960. [8]A famous artist painted a picture of Ruby's first day of school, the picture was on the cover of a magazine.

There are ___ comma splices in the paragraph. Sentences: ___________

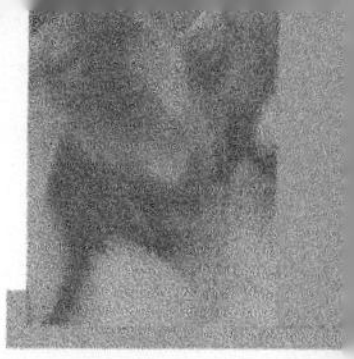

D. Skill Quiz

Check (✓) the correct answer for each item.

1 All complete sentences have
- ☐ a. a subject and more than one clause.
- ☐ b. a subject and a verb.
- ☐ c. a comma and a conjunction.

2 A sentence fragment
- ☐ a. is not a complete sentence.
- ☐ b. is grammatically correct.
- ☐ c. always has a conjunction.

3 A run-on sentence
- ☐ a. does not have a subject or a verb.
- ☐ b. has more than one comma.
- ☐ c. has no comma and no conjunction.

4 A comma splice
- ☐ a. has a conjunction, but no comma.
- ☐ b. has a comma, but no conjunction.
- ☐ c. has a comma and a conjunction.

5 Which of the following is a sentence fragment?
- ☐ a. My parents were teenagers during the Civil Rights Movement.
- ☐ b. After they were born in 1952.
- ☐ c. They fought for civil rights, and they even went to Washington, D.C.

6 Which of the following is a complete sentence?
- ☐ a. Martin Luther King, Jr. was fighting for civil rights.
- ☐ b. He explaining that everyone should be equal.
- ☐ c. Died in 1968, so he was alive when the Civil Rights Act was passed.

7 Which of the following is a run-on sentence?
- ☐ a. Martin Luther King, Jr. gave a speech he was amazing.
- ☐ b. Although he spoke many times in Washington, D.C.
- ☐ c. His speech was inspiring, and it is very famous.

8 Which of the following is a comma splice?
- ☐ a. I never attended a segregated school, but my grandparents did.
- ☐ b. They did not approve of segregation, but it was the law.
- ☐ c. The Civil Rights Act made segregation illegal, it changed many people's lives.

9 Which of the following sentences is correct?
- ☐ a. It hard to understand discrimination.
- ☐ b. We do not think discrimination is fair.
- ☐ c. Want to live in a world with no discrimination.

10 Which of the following sentences is correct?
- ☐ a. Things are better than they were in the past, they could still improve.
- ☐ b. Things are better than they were in the past, but they could still improve.
- ☐ c. Things are better than they were and they could still improve.

30

Irrelevant Information vs. Relevant Information

SLEEP

Connecting to the Theme

When's your best time to study?

What time do you go to bed?
A Before 12 a.m. **B** After 12 a.m.

What time do you get up?
A Before 8 a.m. **B** After 8 a.m.

How do you feel in the morning?
A Ready for the day! **B** Ready for coffee . . .

Mostly As: try to study in the mornings when you are fresh.
Mostly Bs: it looks like evening is the best time for you to study.

A. Skill Presentation

Supporting sentences give more details about the **main idea** of a paragraph, which is often found in the topic sentence.

For example, read this topic sentence and two supporting sentences from a paragraph about college students using energy drinks:

MAIN IDEA

Many college students use energy drinks when they stay up late studying.

Energy drinks are high in caffeine.

The amount of caffeine in these drinks can create unhealthy sleep patterns.

RELEVANT DETAILS

These supporting sentences are directly related to the main idea. It is important that all sentences in a paragraph support the main idea. These details are called **relevant details**.

Now read a third sentence from the same paragraph:

College students eat too much fast food. ✗

The amount of fast food that students eat is not directly related to the main idea. This information is related to health in general, but not specifically to the topic of energy drinks. These details are irrelevant and may confuse the reader. This sentence should not be included in this paragraph.

B. Over to You

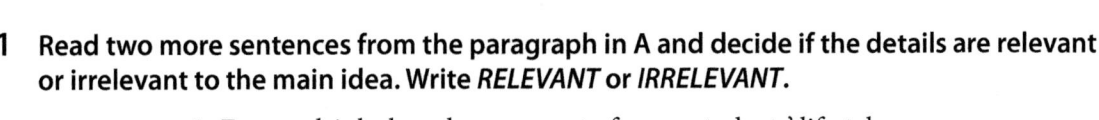

1 Read two more sentences from the paragraph in A and decide if the details are relevant or irrelevant to the main idea. Write *RELEVANT* or *IRRELEVANT*.

_____________ **1** Energy drinks have become part of many students' lifestyles.

_____________ **2** Many students are involved in sports.

2 Read the topic sentence below and the sentences in the chart. Decide if the details are relevant or irrelevant. Check (✓) the box in the correct column.

Topic Sentence: Caffeine is a strong substance that can keep you awake.

	RELEVANT	IRRELEVANT
1. Caffeine is in many energy drinks.		
2. Tim likes the taste of strong coffee.		
3. Caffeine can create unhealthy sleep patterns.		
4. Some tea is made from herbs like mint.		
5. Energy drinks come in many flavors.		
6. If you do not want to stay awake at night, avoid caffeine after 4:00 p.m.		
7. A midnight snack can cause you to gain weight.		
8. A moderate amount of caffeine can help you stay alert.		
9. Some athletes like energy drinks.		
10. Too much caffeine can make it difficult to fall asleep.		
11. Caffeine can be found in cola and chocolate as well as coffee.		
12. There are many different kinds of coffee readily available now.		

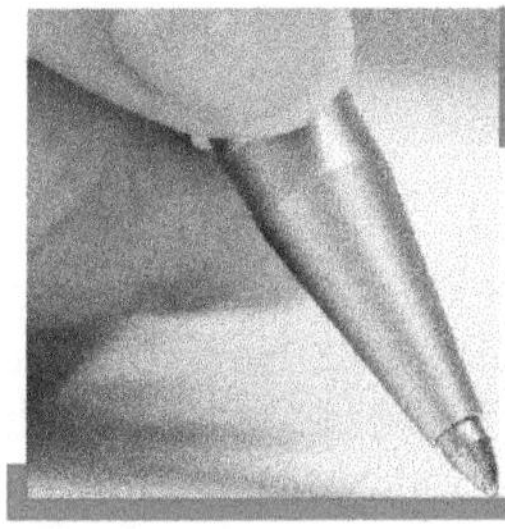

CHECK!

1 All the details in a paragraph must be _____________ to the main idea. That is, they must be directly related to the main idea.

2 Details that do not directly relate to a main idea are called _____________ details. Do not include them in your writing. They may confuse your reader.

C. Practice

1 Read each main idea and write *R* for Relevant or *I* for Irrelevant for each supporting sentence below.

1 Sleep is important.

___ a. We need enough sleep to stay healthy.

___ b. Some people like to sleep late.

2 Babies sleep a lot.

___ a. They keep their parents awake at night.

___ b. A newborn can sleep more than 15 hours in a day.

3 Some people use caffeine to stay awake when they have to work all night.

___ a. They may also consume more caffeine the next day to stay awake.

___ b. Nurses and security guards work hard.

4 Not everyone needs the same amount of sleep.

___ a. Getting up in the middle of the night is a bad habit.

___ b. Some people feel rested after sleeping only a few hours.

5 Energy drinks will help some people stay awake.

___ a. They contain a lot of caffeine.

___ b. They are to blame if someone is unhealthy.

6 Green tea does not usually interfere with sleeping patterns.

___ a. It only contains a small amount of caffeine.

___ b. It may help you lose weight.

7 Most teenagers need more sleep than adults.

___ a. They sometimes stay up late to finish homework.

___ b. Studies show they require at least nine hours per night.

8 Reading a book before bed may help some people fall asleep.

___ a. Some people read magazines on the way to work.

___ b. It helps some people feel relaxed.

2 Read the paragraph and underline the main idea. Then read the supporting sentences again. How many of them are irrelevant?

[1]Eating before bedtime is not necessarily a bad idea. [2]Sleep experts say that some foods can actually make you feel sleepy. [3]However, it is important to choose the right foods. [4]Reading a good book might also relax you. [5]Cherries are an excellent choice to help you sleep. [6]Cherry pie is very easy to make. [7]Bananas are another good option. [8]They naturally help the muscles in the body relax. [9]Stretching can help sore muscles feel better. [10]Two other foods that can help make you sleepy are oatmeal and toast.

There are ___ irrelevant sentences in the paragraph. Sentences: __________

D. Skill Quiz

Check (✓) the correct answer for each item.

1 A supporting detail that is not directly related to the main idea of a paragraph is

☐ a. relevant.
☐ b. irrelevant.
☐ c. necessary for understanding.

2 The main idea of a paragraph is often found in the

☐ a. details.
☐ b. middle.
☐ c. topic sentence.

3 A relevant detail is

☐ a. not important to the main idea.
☐ b. directly related to the main idea.
☐ c. always in the topic sentence.

4 Which supporting sentence is irrelevant to a paragraph about energy drinks and sleep?

☐ a. Energy drinks are high in caffeine.
☐ b. Energy drinks can be expensive.
☐ c. An energy drink may help you stay awake.

5 Which supporting sentence is irrelevant to a paragraph about babies and sleep?

☐ a. Babies grow quickly.
☐ b. Babies need more sleep than adults.
☐ c. A baby can sleep 15 hours in a day.

6 Which supporting sentence is relevant to a paragraph about the benefits of a good night's sleep?

☐ a. Too little sleep can affect driving.
☐ b. Getting enough sleep will improve your mood.
☐ c. Students who do not get enough sleep often fall asleep in class.

7 Which supporting sentence is relevant to a paragraph about food and sleep?

☐ a. Some people believe a cool room is best for sleeping.
☐ b. Some experts claim that cherries can make you sleepy.
☐ c. Some doctors recommend sleeping in a comfortable bed.

8 Which supporting sentence is relevant to a paragraph about caffeine and sleeping patterns?

☐ a. Caffeine may make it difficult to fall asleep.
☐ b. Feeling hungry can wake you up at night.
☐ c. Many teenagers like to sleep late on weekends.

9 A supporting sentence about snacks would likely be found in a paragraph about

☐ a. driving.
☐ b. caffeine.
☐ c. eating patterns.

10 A supporting detail about coffee and tea would likely be found in a paragraph about

☐ a. international foods.
☐ b. caffeine in drinks.
☐ c babies.

31

Transition Words 3: Opinions and Conclusions

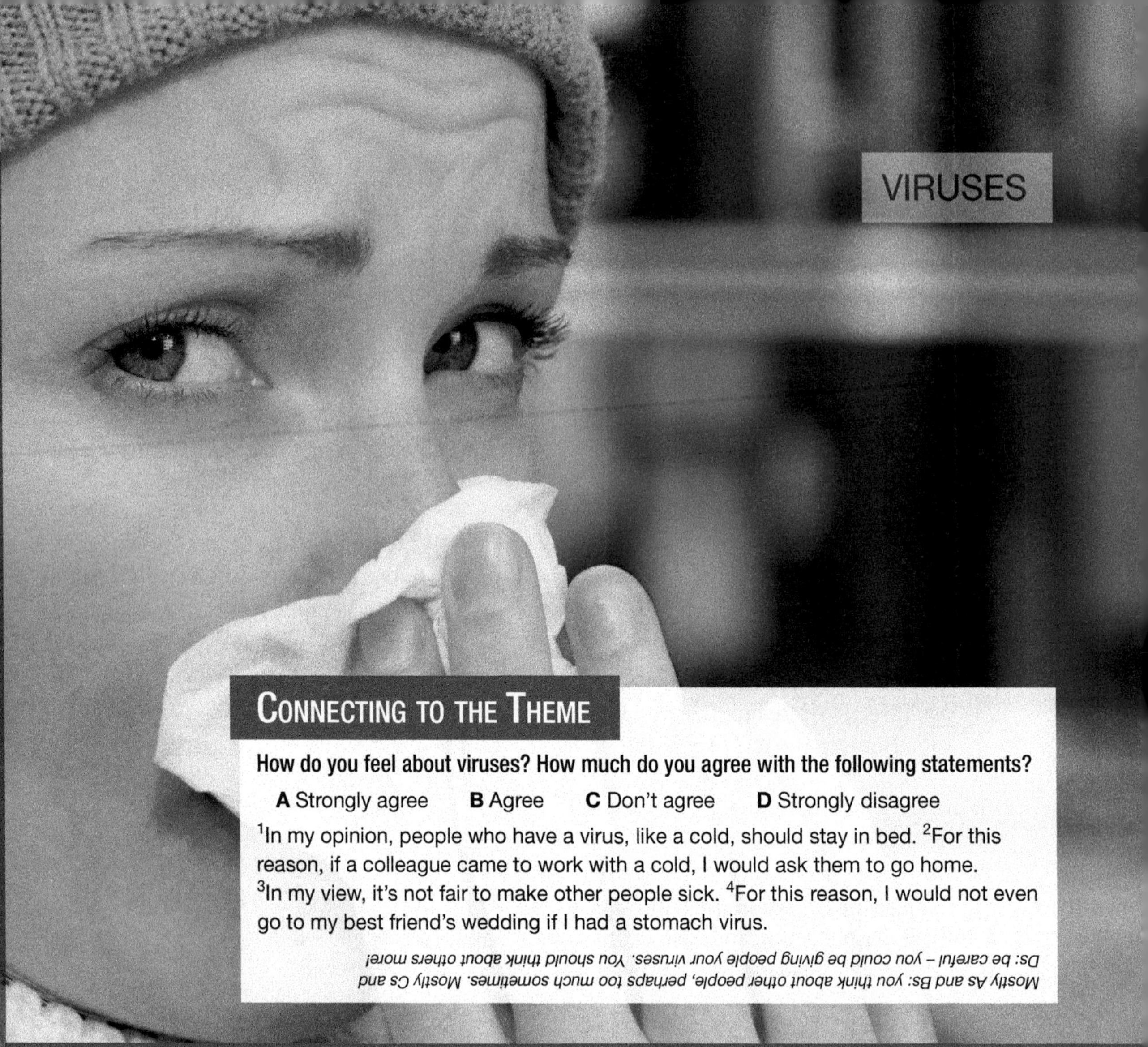

VIRUSES

Connecting to the Theme

How do you feel about viruses? How much do you agree with the following statements?

A Strongly agree **B** Agree **C** Don't agree **D** Strongly disagree

[1]In my opinion, people who have a virus, like a cold, should stay in bed. [2]For this reason, if a colleague came to work with a cold, I would ask them to go home. [3]In my view, it's not fair to make other people sick. [4]For this reason, I would not even go to my best friend's wedding if I had a stomach virus.

Mostly As and Bs: you think about other people, perhaps too much sometimes. Mostly Cs and Ds: be careful – you could be giving people your viruses. You should think about others more!

A. Skill Presentation

Transition words are words that show connections between ideas. They help ideas in a paragraph make sense. They are very important in writing.

When you write about your opinions, there are several transition words that may be useful. Transition words that show an opinion are *in my opinion*, *in my view*, and *most importantly*. Note that *most importantly* shows the reader what you think is the most important or significant idea in your paragraph.

> It is sometimes possible to stop the spread of a virus. In my opinion, one way of doing this is to stay home for at least three days if you are sick.

When you write a concluding sentence, you can use transition words to summarize the facts and opinions in your paragraph. Transition words that show a conclusion are *for this reason*, *for these reasons*, and *in closing*.

> For these reasons, keeping a distance from other people can help prevent the spread of a virus.

Use a comma after these transition words.

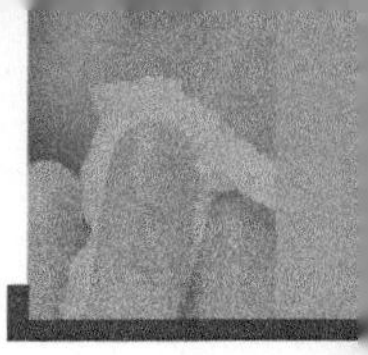

B. Over to You

1 Read the paragraphs about preventing the spread of diseases, and check (✓) the one that shows an opinion. Underline the phrase that introduces the opinion.

☐ **1** Some diseases can be prevented before they become epidemics. In my view, the best way to do this is to wash your hands frequently. Many diseases can be spread by touching. It is, therefore, everyone's responsibility to wash their hands regularly.

☐ **2** Some diseases can be prevented before they become epidemics. Research shows that one good way to do this is to wash your hands frequently. Many diseases can be spread by touching. Experts recommend that everyone wash their hands regularly.

2 Read the sentences about clean water, and check (✓) the one that shows a concluding idea. Underline the phrase that introduces the concluding idea.

☐ **1** For instance, clean water could help prevent epidemics.

☐ **2** In closing, clean water could help prevent epidemics.

3 Read the sentences from paragraphs about epidemics. In each group of sentences, check (✓) three sentences with transitions that show opinions or conclusions.

1
☐ a. Many viruses come from animals.
☐ b. Animals that are infected with a virus sometimes spread the virus to humans.
☐ c. This can lead to an epidemic.
☐ d. In my opinion, people need to be careful when they work with animals.
☐ e. Most importantly, there should be laws about how people work with animals.
☐ f. Studies show this can help stop viruses from spreading.
☐ g. In closing, laws and education could help prevent epidemics.

2
☐ a. The Centers for Disease Control and Prevention (CDC) helps people understand epidemics.
☐ b. In my view, the CDC has done an excellent job of educating people.
☐ c. However, many people still die each year from preventable illnesses.
☐ d. In my opinion, even more education would help.
☐ e. For this reason, the CDC needs to create more programs to fight the spread of disease.

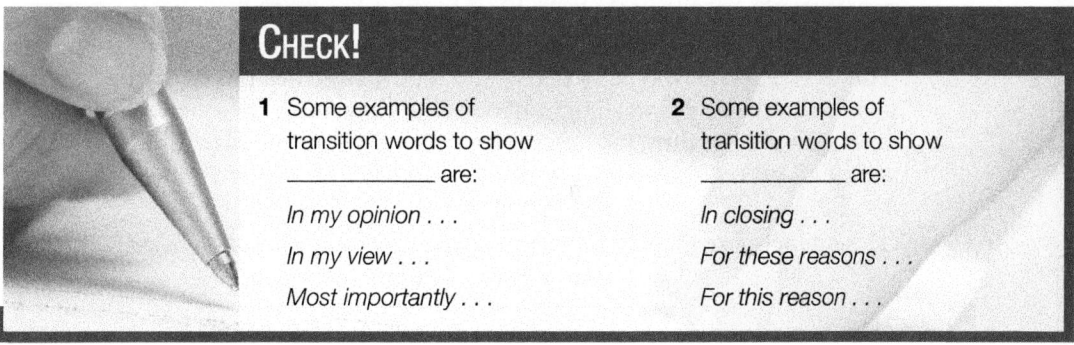

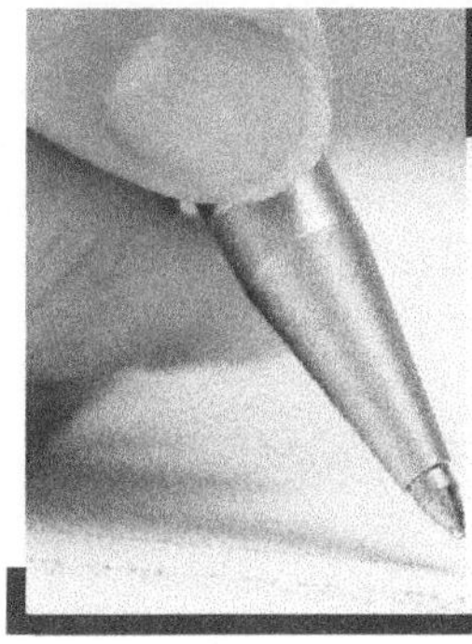

CHECK!

1 Some examples of transition words to show ____________ are:

In my opinion . . .

In my view . . .

Most importantly . . .

2 Some examples of transition words to show ____________ are:

In closing . . .

For these reasons . . .

For this reason . . .

C. Practice

1 Read each sentence in the chart. Decide if it expresses an opinion or a concluding idea. Check (✓) the box in the correct column.

	OPINION	CONCLUDING IDEA
1. In my opinion, sick people should not travel on planes.		
2. In my opinion, diseases would not spread if sick people never traveled.		
3. For these reasons, airlines need strict rules about sick passengers.		
4. In my view, everyone should get a flu shot.		
5. Most importantly, flu shots should be free.		
6. In closing, there would be fewer flu epidemics if more people got flu shots.		
7. In my view, it is better for children to stay home when they are sick.		
8. For this reason, illnesses spread easily in schools.		
9. Most importantly, employees should wash their hands before returning to work.		
10. In closing, more schools should excuse students from school if they are sick.		

2 The supporting sentences in these paragraphs show opinions. How many sentences use incorrect transitions to show opinions? Underline the incorrect transitions.

1 [1]Some people use liquid hand gel to clean their hands. [2]Next, washing your hands with soap is better than using liquid hand gel. [3]In my view, using liquid hand gel is a good way to prevent viral infections. [4]In contrast, there should be liquid hand gel in all classrooms. [5]Most importantly, people should wash their hands before they serve food. [6]In closing, employees should wear gloves when they prepare food.

___ sentences use incorrect transitions to show opinions. Sentences: ___________

2 [1]Animals sometimes carry diseases. [2]In my view, people with pets should be careful. [3]However, anyone who has a pet should follow basic health safety rules. [4]In my opinion, people should always wash their hands after they touch their pets. [5]Then, they should keep their pets healthy, too. [6]For these reasons, people need to take their pets to veterinarians regularly.

___ sentences use incorrect transitions to show opinions. Sentences: ___________

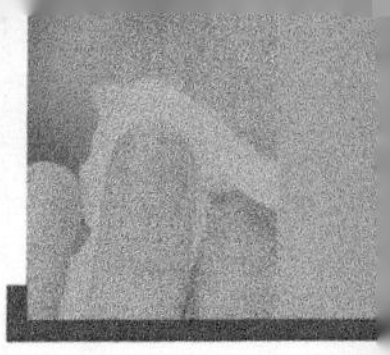

D. Skill Quiz

Check (✓) the correct answer for each item.

1 Transition words

☐ a. connect ideas in writing.
☐ b. combine independent clauses.
☐ c. express action.

2 When should you use transition words that show an opinion?

☐ a. when you want to give the steps of a process
☐ b. when you want to write what you think about a topic
☐ c. when you want to give an example of something

3 Which transition shows your most significant idea?

☐ a. Most importantly . . .
☐ b. In my opinion . . .
☐ c. In closing . . .

4 Which transition shows a concluding idea?

☐ a. In my view . . .
☐ b. Most importantly . . .
☐ c. For these reasons . . .

5 Which sentence gives an opinion?

☐ a. In my house, we wash our hands after we eat.
☐ b. In my view, you should wash your hands often.
☐ c. For this reason, we wash our hands before dinner.

6 Which sentence gives a concluding idea?

☐ a. I believe that face masks could prevent epidemics.
☐ b. Face masks are inexpensive.
☐ c. In closing, everyone should wear face masks when traveling.

7 Which sentence uses a comma correctly?

☐ a. I believe, epidemics are difficult to prevent.
☐ b. In my opinion, a few changes could stop pandemics.
☐ c. I think that, the swine flu was the worst epidemic of the decade.

8 Which sentence is correct without a comma?

☐ a. I believe that young children should not get vaccines.
☐ b. Most importantly elderly people should get vaccines.
☐ c. In closing the hospitals should give free vaccines.

9 Choose the sentence that gives an opinion about this statement: *There are many simple things people could do to prevent epidemics.*

☐ a. For example, in my view, sick children should stay home from school.
☐ b. I believe that more hospitals should be built around the world.
☐ c. For this reason, infected people should live their lives normally.

10 Choose the sentence that gives a concluding idea about this topic: *Many viruses can be prevented with healthy habits.*

☐ a. Viruses can cause diseases.
☐ b. For this reason, people should exercise and eat healthy food.
☐ c. In my view, it is hard to work in a hospital.

32 The Essay

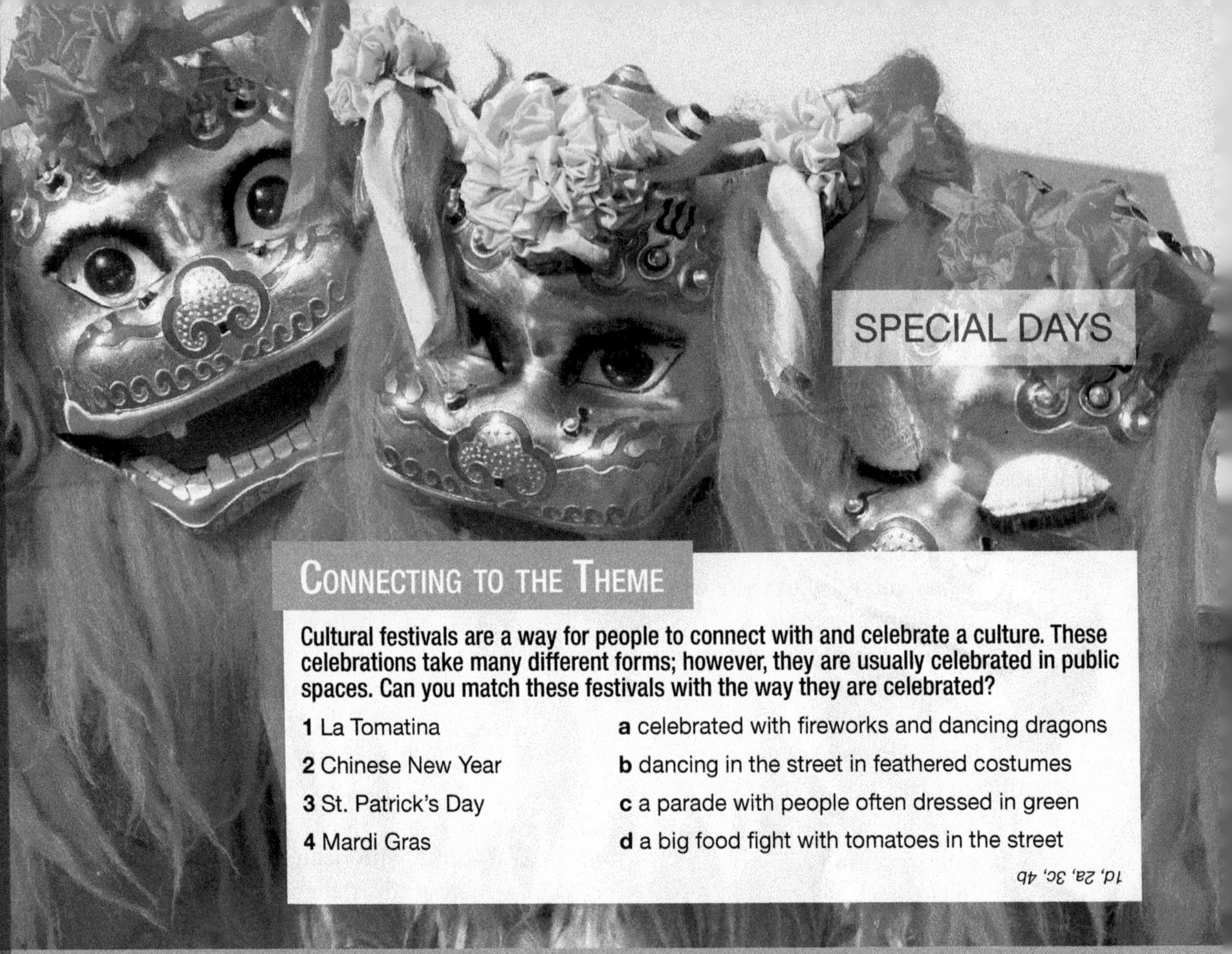

SPECIAL DAYS

Connecting to the Theme

Cultural festivals are a way for people to connect with and celebrate a culture. These celebrations take many different forms; however, they are usually celebrated in public spaces. Can you match these festivals with the way they are celebrated?

1 La Tomatina	**a** celebrated with fireworks and dancing dragons
2 Chinese New Year	**b** dancing in the street in feathered costumes
3 St. Patrick's Day	**c** a parade with people often dressed in green
4 Mardi Gras	**d** a big food fight with tomatoes in the street

1d, 2a, 3c, 4b

A. Skill Presentation

A group of related paragraphs about one topic is called an **essay**. An essay has a broader focus than a paragraph, but the structure is very similar.

The main idea of an essay is usually in the **thesis statement**. The thesis statement is usually the last sentence of the introductory paragraph. Many thesis statements give two or three **examples**. Each example is then explained in its own supporting paragraph. In this way, the thesis statement can also show how the essay is organized. An essay always has a **concluding paragraph** that restates the main idea. Look at this excerpt from an essay about Mother's Day.

Mothers everywhere deserve a day of recognition. More than 46 countries have a Mother's Day holiday. However, different countries celebrate the holiday in different ways. [TS]The [1]United Kingdom, [2]Mexico, and [3]Indonesia have some interesting similarities and differences in celebrating Mother's Day.

[1]Many believe that Mother's Day began in the United States, but it actually started hundreds of years ago in the United Kingdom. . . .

[2]Mexico also has some unique ways of celebrating Mother's Day. . . .

[3]Another country with interesting Mother's Day traditions is Indonesia. . . .

[CP]There are both similarities and differences among these three countries' Mother's Day celebrations. The United Kingdom, Mexico, and Indonesia all celebrate Mother's Day in slightly different ways. However, they also have things in common. Flowers are the most popular gift, and children often prepare food for their mothers. In all three countries, families usually try to help mothers relax on this day. For Mother's Day around the world, the most important idea is to show gratitude and respect to mothers.

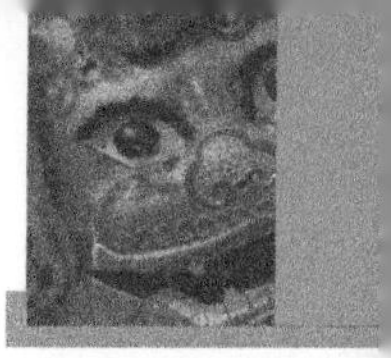

B. Over to You

1 Look at the sentences in bold below. Circle the correct answers.

1 Sentence 1 is *a thesis statement* | *a supporting sentence* | *a topic sentence.*

2 Sentence 2 is *a concluding sentence* | *thesis statement* | *topic sentence.*

3 Sentence 3 is *a thesis statement* | *a concluding sentence* | *a background information.*

4 Paragraph 4 is *a concluding paragraph* | *an introductory paragraph* | *a supporting paragraph.*

5 The sentences in 5 are *supporting sentences* | *topic sentences* | *concluding sentences.*

6 Paragraph 6 is *an introductory paragraph* | *a concluding paragraph* | *a supporting paragraph.*

Mother's Day

Mothers everywhere deserve a day of recognition. More than 46 countries have a Mother's Day holiday. However, different countries celebrate the holiday in different ways. [1]**The United Kingdom, Mexico, and Indonesia have some interesting similarities and differences in celebrating Mother's Day.**

[2]**Many believe that Mother's Day began in the United States, but it actually started hundreds of years ago in the United Kingdom.** Around the 1600s, England became the first country to make a special day for mothers. It was originally called "Mothering Sunday," but now everyone calls it Mother's Day. Families give gifts and visit each other. Some people also bake a special almond cake for their mothers. [3]**There is a lot of interesting history and tradition around Mother's Day in the United Kingdom.**

[4]**Mexico also has some unique ways of celebrating Mother's Day. Many children sing songs to their mothers. The most popular gift is flowers, but there are some other interesting traditions, too. Children make homemade gifts for their mothers. There are also special services in churches. The Mexican Mother's Day celebration is a very important event.**

Another country with interesting Mother's Day traditions is Indonesia. [5]**Some Indonesians have surprise parties for their mothers. Many people also have cooking competitions. However, mothers do not have to do chores. Like Mexico and the United Kingdom, children usually give gifts, such as flowers, to their mothers.** Many Indonesian mothers enjoy a very relaxing Mother's Day.

[6]**There are both similarities and differences among these three countries' Mother's Day celebrations. The United Kingdom, Mexico, and Indonesia all celebrate Mother's Day in slightly different ways. However, they also have many things in common. Flowers are the most popular gift, and children often prepare food for their mothers. In all three countries, families usually try to help mothers relax on this day. For Mother's Day around the world, the most important idea is to show gratitude and respect to mothers.**

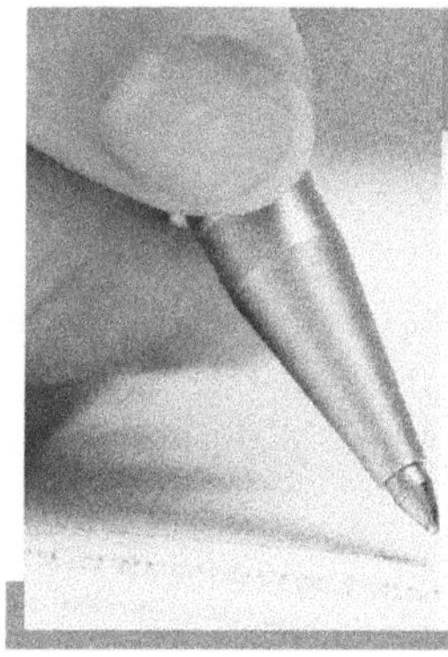

CHECK!

1 An essay has several paragraphs about one topic, and it includes a ____________ statement.

2 The thesis statement gives the ____________ idea of the essay. Many thesis statements give three examples, and each example is explained in its own supporting ____________.

3 The thesis statement can also show how the essay is organized. It is usually the ____________ sentence in the introductory paragraph.

C. Practice

1 Each pair of sentences (1–3) in the chart comes from a different essay. Within each pair, decide which of the sentences (a or b) is the thesis statement, and which is a topic sentence from a body paragraph. Check (✓) the box in the correct column.

	TOPIC SENTENCE	THESIS STATEMENT
1. **Essay Topic:** *Earth Day*		
a. In countries such as Canada, Earth Day provides an opportunity to teach children about the environment.		
b. Earth Day celebrations include education, volunteering, and community service.		
2. **Essay Topic:** *Family celebrations*		
a. Many nations have created special holidays to celebrate mothers, fathers, grandparents, and children.		
b. Father's Day is one special holiday for celebrating family members.		
3. **Essay Topic:** *Cinco de Mayo*		
a. Many people celebrate Cinco de Mayo, but not everyone understands its social, cultural, and historic importance.		
b. For the people of Mexico, the traditions of Cinco de Mayo are closely connected with the past.		

2 Check (✓) the best thesis statement for each essay topic.

1 Earth Day celebrations

- ☐ a. Earth Day is in April.
- ☐ b. The science building has a rooftop garden.
- ☐ c. On Earth Day, people can help their communities, the environment, and the world.

2 Black Friday

- ☐ a. Black Friday helps retailers attract customers, sell products, and make larger profits.
- ☐ b. Black Friday is after Thanksgiving.
- ☐ c. The holiday shopping season is busy.

3 Independence Day celebrations

- ☐ a. People love to have picnics on Independence Day.
- ☐ b. Picnics, parades, and fireworks are just a few ways that communities celebrate Independence Day.
- ☐ c. Fireworks on Independence Day can be dangerous.

D. Skill Quiz

Check (✓) the correct answer for each item.

1 The topic sentence in a paragraph is usually the ___ sentence.

- ☐ a. first
- ☐ b. second
- ☐ c. last

2 An essay is usually ___ a paragraph.

- ☐ a. narrower than
- ☐ b. broader than
- ☐ c. better than

3 Essays are usually ___ paragraphs.

- ☐ a. the same length as
- ☐ b. shorter than
- ☐ c. longer than

4 The thesis statement in an essay is often the ___ sentence in the introductory paragraph.

- ☐ a. first
- ☐ b. last
- ☐ c. second

5 Choose the thesis statement for an essay about retailers during holidays.

- ☐ a. Retailers offer special deals to attract more customers and increase profits around holidays.
- ☐ b. One store had a big sale a few weeks ago.
- ☐ c. The day after Thanksgiving is called Black Friday.

6 Choose the topic sentence from a paragraph about Father's Day gifts.

- ☐ a. Father's Day is celebrated all over the world, and it often honors grandfathers as well as fathers.
- ☐ b. Some people cook at home for Father's Day, but others choose to celebrate by taking their father to a restaurant.
- ☐ c. For fathers who have special interests, many people choose to give their father something useful.

7 Choose the topic sentence from a paragraph about Valentine's Day gifts.

- ☐ a. Most stores offer special deals on gifts like chocolate, red roses, and fine jewelry to attract Valentine's Day customers.
- ☐ b. For example, retailers may advertise great offers for roses and chocolate; however, fine jewelry might still be very expensive.
- ☐ c. Buyers need to pay attention to prices.

8 Choose the thesis statement from an introductory paragraph about holiday decorations in department stores.

- ☐ a. It is fun to see seasonal holiday decorations in department stores.
- ☐ b. Some retailers plan big displays well in advance.
- ☐ c. These stores believe that creative holiday decorations will make shopping exciting, attract customers, and increase profits.

Glossary of Writing Terms

academic writing: writing for school; it usually includes more formal language than other kinds of writing (See Skill 28.)

adjective clause (also called a *relative clause*)**:** a dependent clause that describes or gives more information about a noun; it often starts with *that, which,* or *who* (See Skill 12.)

apostrophe: a punctuation mark (') used in contractions or before or after *-s* to show possession (See Skill 28.)

argument: a statement of opinion about an idea that is supported by facts (See Skill 25.)

auxiliary verb: a verb such as *do* or *be* that is used before a main verb in a sentence (See Skill 8.)

capitalize: to make the first letter of a word into a capital letter (See Skill 4.)

capital letter: the form of a letter used to begin sentences and proper nouns; it is usually bigger than a lowercase letter (See Skill 4.)

chronological order: the order in which events happen in time (See Skill 19.)

clause: a group of words that has a subject and a verb (See Skill 7.)

comma: a punctuation mark (,) used in writing to separate certain clauses in a sentence or to separate three or more items in a list (See Skill 5.)

comma splice: two or more independent clauses connected only by a comma (See Skill 7.)

complex sentence: a sentence with an independent clause and a dependent clause connected by a conjunction, such as *after, because, if,* or *when* (See Skill 14.)

compound sentence: a sentence with two independent clauses connected by a comma and a conjunction, such as *and, or, but,* or *so* (See Skill 13.)

concluding paragraph: the last paragraph in an essay; it restates the main idea (See Skill 32.)

concluding sentence: a sentence that restates the main idea in a paragraph using different words than the topic sentence; it is usually the last sentence in a paragraph (See Skill 11.)

conjunction: a word such as *and, or, so,* or *but* that connects single words, phrases, or clauses (See Skill 7.)

contraction: a shortened form of a word or combination of words; it uses an apostrophe (See Skill 28.)

counterargument: a statement of opinion that is different from the writer's opinion expressed in the argument (See Skill 25.)

dependent clause: a clause that cannot be used alone as a complete sentence; it has a subject and verb but does not express a complete idea (See Skill 12.)

descriptive adjective: a word such as *large, friendly,* or *talkative* that gives specific information about a noun (See Skill 21.)

detail: a specific fact or piece of information (See Skill 16.)

essay: a group of paragraphs about one topic (See Skill 32.)

example: something that illustrates a rule (See Skill 10.)

fact: something that is true and can be proven (See Skill 24.)

formal: a style of writing used when it is not appropriate to show familiarity, such as in business; a college essay is an example of formal writing (See Skill 27.)

formatting: the way a piece of writing is shown or arranged; paragraph formatting includes indentation and space between sentences; outline formatting includes letters, numbers, and indentation to help organize ideas (See Skill 2.)

general statement: a statement that is not specific; it is broad and does not give details (See Skill 16.)

indent: to add space before the first word in a paragraph (See Skill 2.)

independent clause: a group of words that has a subject and a verb and expresses a complete idea; it can be used alone as a complete sentence (See Skill 7.)

informal: a style of writing used with friends, family, and children; a personal e-mail or text message is an example of informal writing (See Skill 27.)

introductory paragraph: the first paragraph in an essay; it tells what the essay is about (See Skill 32.)

irrelevant details: details that are not directly related to the main idea in a paragraph (See Skill 30.)

lowercase letter: the small form of a letter (See Skill 4.)

main idea: the most important thought about a topic in a paragraph or essay (See Skill 9.)

noun: a word for a person, place, thing, or idea (See Skill 3.)

opinion: a belief that cannot be proven (See Skill 24.)

outline: a summary of a piece of writing that helps organize ideas and has special formatting (See Skill 22.)

paragraph: a group of sentences about one topic; it has special formatting (See Skill 2.)

period: a punctuation mark (.) used to show where the end of a sentence is (See Skill 5.)

phrase: a group of words that forms part of a sentence (See Skill 17.)

plural subject: a subject in a sentence that has two or more nouns connected by *and* or a subject that refers to more than one person, place, thing, or idea (See Skill 3.)

plural verb: the form of a verb that agrees with a plural subject (See Skill 3.)

pronoun: a word that is used in place of a noun (See Skill 6.)

proper noun: the name of a specific person, place, or thing; it is capitalized (See Skill 4.)

punctuation: special marks that are used to show the divisions between phrases and sentences (See Skill 5.)

quantifier: a word or phrase such as *many*, *much*, and *a lot* that shows the amount of something (See Skill 16.)

question: a sentence that asks for information (See Skill 5.)

question mark: a punctuation mark (?) used at the end of a sentence to show that it is a question (See Skill 5.)

refutation: a response to a counterargument that strengthens the writer's opinion expressed in the argument (See Skill 25.)

relative clause (also called an adjective clause): a dependent clause that describes or gives more information about a noun; it often starts with *that*, *which*, or *who* (See Skill 12.)

relevant details: details that are directly related to the main idea in a paragraph (See Skill 30.)

run-on sentence: two or more independent clauses connected without a comma or a conjunction (See Skill 7.)

second-person pronoun: a pronoun such as *you* that a person uses when writing to someone else (See Skill 28.)

sentence: a group of words that has a subject and a verb and expresses a complete idea (See Skill 1.)

sentence fragment: a group of words that does not include a subject and a verb or does not express a complete idea; a dependent clause by itself is a sentence fragment (See Skill 8.)

sentence variety: using different types of sentences, such as compound, complex, and simple sentences, to add interest to your writing and to make it more academic (See Skill 15.)

simple sentence: a sentence with exactly one independent clause (See Skill 1.)

singular subject: a subject in a sentence that refers to only one person, place, thing, or idea (See Skill 3.)

singular verb: the form of a verb that agrees with a singular subject (See Skill 3.)

statement: a sentence that gives information (See Skill 5.)

subject: the person, place, thing, or idea that comes before the verb in a statement (See Skill 1.)

subject pronoun: a word that is used in place of a noun that is a subject in a sentence (See Skill 6.)

subject–verb agreement: agreement in number between a subject and verb; a singular subject is matched with a singular verb, and a plural subject is matched with a plural verb (See Skill 3.)

subordinating conjunction: a conjunction such as *after*, *because*, *if*, and *when* that joins a dependent clause to an independent clause in a complex sentence (See Skill 14.)

summarize: to briefly state the most important information in a piece of writing (See Skill 22.)

supporting sentence: a sentence that gives more details about the main idea in a paragraph (See Skill 10.)

tense: the form of a verb that shows past or present time (See Skill 20.)

thesis statement: a statement that gives the main idea of an essay (See Skill 32.)

third-person pronoun: a pronoun such as *he*, *him*, or *they* that a person uses when writing about other people (See Skill 28.)

time clause: a word or phrase that shows the order of events and begins with a time word such as *before*, *after*, *when*, *while*, or *as soon as* (See Skill 17.)

time expression: a phrase that tells when something happened or will happen (See Skill 17.)

topic: what is being written about (See Skill 2.)

topic sentence: a sentence that expresses the main idea of a paragraph and is often the first sentence in a paragraph (See Skill 9.)

transition words: words such as *next*, *for example*, or *in addition* that show connections between ideas and help ideas in a paragraph make sense; they usually come first in a sentence and are followed by a comma (See Skill 19.)

verb: a word that describes an action or a state; it tells what the subject in a sentence is doing or being (See Skill 1.)

Academic Word List

What are the most common words in academic English? Which words appear most frequently in readings in different academic subject areas? Dr. Averil Coxhead, who is currently a Senior Lecturer at Victoria University of Wellington in New Zealand, did research to try to answer this question. The result was the **Academic Word List** (AWL), a list of 570 words or word families that appear in academic readings in many different academic fields. These words are extremely useful for students to know. In *Skills for Effective Writing*, you will encounter a number of these words in context.

The following is a list of the AWL words in *Skills for Effective Writing 2* and the Skills where they appear.

academic	9; 15–16; 24; 27–28
access	8
accommodation	25
achieve	9; 16; 28
acknowledge	25
administration	18
adult	1; 5; 26; 28; 30
affect	1–2; 17–18; 18; 22–23; 26; 28; 30
affected	27
aid	5; 10; 28
alternative	16
analytical	18
approach	22
appropriate	3; 21; 27
area	11; 13; 18; 27
assess	21
assign	14
assignment	3; 20; 24
attitude	21
available	5; 30
benefit	10; 20; 30
brief	3
briefly	22–23
challenge	9; 29
challenging	9; 27
chart	1; 3; 5; 7–8; 10; 12–17; 19; 21; 23–24; 26; 28–32
chemical	2; 10; 13; 15; 28
civil	29
clause	7; 12–15; 17; 23; 29; 31
colleague	8; 13; 31
comment	1; 8
communicate	3; 8; 18
communication	3; 18
community	20; 26; 32
complex	14–15; 23
complexity	15
compound	13–15; 17; 23; 29
computer	2–4; 6; 8; 13; 19; 26
concluding	2; 9; 10–11; 22; 31–32
conclusion	10–11; 31
conference	1
consistency	20
consistent	6; 20
consistently	6
consume	30
consumer	22
contact	3–4; 21
context	27
contrast	26; 31
contrasting	26
contribute	10
contribution	25
convince	22
co-ordinating	15
create	4; 6–7; 9; 11; 14–15; 22; 27; 29; 30–32
creative	22; 32
credit	7; 18; 25
cultural	32
culture	32
cycle	28
decade	6; 23; 26; 31
declining	23